D1143458

AD 04210221

modern classics

modern classics

Knit Over Twenty Timeless Designs

Louisa Harding

COLLINS & BROWN

LINCOLNSHIRE
COUNTY COUNCIL

First published in the United Kingdom in 2006 by

Collins & Brown

151 Freston Road

London W10 6TH

An imprint of Anova Books Company Ltd

Copyright © 2006 Collins & Brown Limited

Text © 2006 Louisa Harding

The right of Louisa Harding to be identified as the author of this

work has been asserted by her in accordance with the

Copyright, Designs and Patents Act, 1988.

All rights reserved. No part of this publication may be repro-

duced, stored in a retrieval system, or transmitted in any form or

by any means electronic, mechanical, photocopying, recording

or otherwise, without the prior written permission of the copy-

right owner.

Commissioning Editors: **Michelle Lo and Marie Clayton**

Design Manager: **Gemma Wilson**

Designer: **Louise Leffler**

Senior Production Controller: **Morna McPherson**

Photographed by **Marco Micceri**

Stylist: **Ella Bradley**

Editor: **Marie Clayton**

Illustrator: **Kang Chen**

Pattern checker: **Penny Hill**

ISBN 1 84340 297 1

A CIP catalogue record for this book is available from the British

Library.

10 9 8 7 6 5 4 3 2 1

Reproduction by Anorax

Printed and bound by Kyodo, Singapore

This book can be ordered direct from the publisher.

Contact the marketing department, but try your bookshop first.

www.anovabooks.com

contents

introduction

modern – *contemporary, current, up to date, recent, new, present, fresh*
classic – *timeless, immortal, unforgettable, memorable, lasting, ageless*

These are the definitions given for the words modern and classic. These words are opposites. So why call a book *Modern Classics*?

The idea for this book was to produce a collection of classic hand knitwear designs, designs that never date. The sweater or cardigan that you want as the constant in your wardrobe, the one you can pull on knowing that it will feel comfortable. In turn it will make you feel comfortable and confident when wearing it. The modern element comes from the up-to-the-minute yarns that are used.

For all women, clothes are a vital element of our psyche. We place great importance on what we wear and how we feel when we wear a certain garment. When we knit we feel a spiritualness in being able to create something new from such simple tools. To craft a beautiful garment out of a ball of yarn and two pointed sticks combines these two elements of our psyche and spirit, to create a harmony, in itself a very "modern classic" thought.

In this book I hope you will find a design or two that appeals to your taste and sparks your creativity.

I have designed a varied selection of classic garment shapes: sweaters, cardigans, jumpers and jackets. Some designs are knit in simple stocking stitch, ideal for the beginner or returning knitter. Other designs use a variety of different techniques, including Fair Isle, cable, and lace stitch patterns. Some are easy, some are for the more accomplished knitter. To enhance the modern element, I have knitted the garments using a diverse selection of yarns from my own yarn line, which are the result of some of the most up-to-date spinning technology, combining fibres and textures. These in turn are constructed and dyed to produce a beautifully feminine colour palette.

Femininity is very important to the essence of this book; it is important that we think about ourselves in terms of shape when choosing a design to knit. The idea of a classic garment is that the silhouette will never date, but the shape has to suit your figure. You will enjoy wearing what you create if it is the correct shape for you.

If curvy, we should wear clothes that accentuate those curves and make us feel feminine and confident. If we are straight with little waist definition, then wearing clothes that have elegant lines and drape will make you feel poised and self assured.

To help you choose which design to knit, a size indication is given at the beginning of every pattern. All body shapes vary and the way we like to wear our clothes varies so make sure you choose the right garment size. Do this by measuring an item of your own clothing that you like the fit of, then choose the instruction size accordingly. Choose a yarn you like the feel of, in a colour that inspires you and coordinates with the items in your wardrobe. Then, after many hours of lovingly knitting and finishing, you will have a beautiful timeless garment that you will enjoy wearing for many years, a "Modern Classic."

how to use this book

This book is designed to appeal to wide range of knitters, so I have included projects for those just picking up their needles for the first time, returning knitters and those with more experience. I have included some basic knitting techniques used in the book on page 14. In this section you will also find details on how to finish your project beautifully, including pressing and sewing, as well as instructions on knitting from charts, knitting lace, cables, Fair Isle and textured patterns.

THE KNITTING PATTERNS

Each pattern has written instructions. We have tried to make the patterns as simple as possible and they are laid out as follows:

Materials – Here you are given a list of all the ingredients that are needed to complete your chosen project.

Yarn – This indicates the amount of yarn needed to complete the design. All projects that use more than one colour of yarn will have the amount needed for each shade.

Needles – Listed here are the suggested knitting needles used to make the project. The smaller needles are usually used for edgings or ribs, the larger needles for the main body fabric.

Buttons – When buttons are needed to finish your project, the quantity and size needed are specified here.

Tension – Tension is the single most important factor when you begin knitting. The fabric tension is written something like this: 20 sts and 28 rows = 10 cm (4 in.) measured over stocking stitch using size 4 mm (US 6) needles. Each pattern is worked out mathematically, so if the correct tension is not achieved the project will not fit as intended. Before beginning to knit your garment we recommend you check your tension as follows: Using the needle size given, cast on 5-10 more stitches than stated in the tension, and work 5-10 more rows. When you have knitted your tension square, lay it on a flat surface, place a ruler or tape measure horizontally, and count the number of stitches equal to the distance of 10 cm (4 in.). Then place the measure vertically and count the number of rows. These two should both equal the tension given in the pattern. If you have

too many stitches to 10 cm (4 in.), try again using a larger size needle, if you have too few stitches to 10 cm (4 in.) use a smaller size needle. Note: Check your tension regularly as you knit, as once you become relaxed and confident with your knitting, your tension can change. Some of the patterns are knitted in rib, textured pattern, or with cables and it is quite difficult to measure the tension of these patterns as they are meant to have an elastic fit. The pattern will specify whether the tension swatch should be knitted in pattern or stocking stitch.

Sizes – The sizes are given in the table at the beginning of every pattern. As all body shapes vary and the way we like to wear our clothes varies, make sure that you choose the right garment size by measuring an item of your own clothing that fits well, and choose the instruction size accordingly.

Measurements – I've included the standard measurements for the actual width at under arm, the finished length, and the sleeve length to under arm where applicable. A letter next to each measurement is also referenced in the schematic.

Abbreviations – To keep patterns to a manageable length, abbreviations are used for some terms. A full list of abbreviations can be found on page 120. These may look confusing if you are not used to them, so it may be a good idea to photocopy that list and keep it next to you while knitting.

Skill Levels – I have included projects for knitters of all skill levels and indicated them as such:

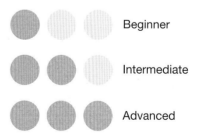

Beginner

Intermediate

Advanced

yarn information

Yarn can be purchased in two different ways: from the yarn shop, where you will find really helpful, knowledgeable staff and an amazing array of products, knitting yarns, needles, buttons, and books; and from the Internet.

I recommend that you visit a good yarn store when you first start knitting. You can get an idea of what is offered, and touch and feel a ball of yarn. You will find an amazing array of colour and texture – the choice is unbelievable and you will feel like a child in a candy store, so choosing which one to use can be quite daunting.

There are many really good Internet yarn sites, which you can find easily when you search for knitting yarns. They have lots of information and are a fantastic resource – you can order colour cards and other products. Once you know what you are looking for, the Internet is generally a reliable way of purchasing your yarns.

For the patterns in this book, I have specified the yarns that I have used – all are included in my own yarn line. I have personally chosen all the yarns for their unique and individual qualities and selected the colors so that they all coordinate.

This is a simple summary of yarn types that are available:
Wool comes from the fleece of a sheep and is the traditional yarn for knitting. Wool is very warm to wear, as it holds in the heat. Traditionally wool can be itchy and scratchy when you wear it next to the skin. Many yarn spinners now make very soft wool blends, combining wool with other fibers to create colour and texture.
Cotton yarns are made from the cotton plant and are now very popular. The yarn is soft and not itchy on sensitive skins, but it does not have much elasticity. It also can be quite heavy, so it is essential that the correct tension is achieved to avoid the garment pulling out of shape.

Wool-and-Cotton Blend is a good compromise with the softness of cotton but the properties of wool, retaining warmth and elasticity.
Wool-and-Cashmere Blend feels wonderful to touch and wear. Pure cashmere is a luxury fibre and can be expensive, so many spinners combine it with wool to make it more affordable.
Silk is a wonderful fibre that absorbs colour when it is dyed to produce beautiful vivid shades. It is expensive to produce and is often mixed with other yarn fibres.
Angora, which comes from the Angora rabbit, is a soft, fluffy and warm fibre that is often blended with wool to create unique effects.
Mohair comes form the Angora goat. When spun it produces a light, fluffy, and very warm yarn, and because it is hairy you can knit it to the same tension as a thicker yarn using bigger needles, as the hairy fibres give the fabric stability.
Synthetic yarns made from man-made fibres come in many varieties, so you can easily find exciting experimental yarns in wonderful colours. They are great as fun items but will not have the long lasting properties of natural yarns.

SUBSTITUTING YARNS

I have designed the projects in this book using the specific yarns that are detailed, but you may wish to substitute a yarn I have used for one of your own choice. Please take great care if you do this, as all the patterns in this book are worked out mathematically to the specified yarn. If you substitute a yarn you must achieve exactly the same tension stated in the pattern or your project will turn out too big or too small. Look out for a similar yarn with the same tension – this will be stated on the label. I suggest that to check the tension you knit a sample swatch of your chosen yarn before embarking on the design. Despite saying this, it can be great fun to substitute yarns and it will certainly start you thinking creatively about knitting.

techniques

BASIC KNITTING INSTRUCTIONS

With a basic knowledge of the simplest stitches you can create your own unique hand-knitted garments. When you begin to knit, you will feel very clumsy, all fingers and thumbs, but this stage passes as confidence and experience grows. Many people are put off by hand knitting because they feel that they are not using the correct techniques to hold the needles, yarn or work the stitches, but all knitters develop their own style, so please persevere.

CASTING ON

This is the term used for making a foundation row of stitches, which is used for each piece of knitting. First make a slip knot and slip this onto a needle. This is the basis for the casting-on techniques described below.

Thumb Cast On – This method uses only one needle and gives a neat, but elastic edge. Make a slip knot approximately 1 meter (1 yard) from the cut end of the yarn – you use this length to cast on the stitches. For a knitted piece, the length between the cut end and the slip knot can be difficult to judge, but allow approximately three times the width measurement.

HOW TO KNIT

The knit stitch is the simplest to learn. If you knit every row you create garter stitch, which is the simplest of all knitted fabrics.

HOW TO PURL

The purl stitch is a little more complicated to master. Using a combination of knit and purl stitches together forms the basis of most knitted fabrics. When you knit one row, then purl one row, you create stocking stitch, the most common knitted fabric.

JOINING IN A NEW YARN

A new ball of yarn can be joined in on either a right side or a wrong side row, but to give a neat finish it is important that you join it at the start of a row. Simply drop the old yarn, start knitting with the new ball, then after a few stitches tie the two ends together in a temporary knot. These ends are then sewn into the knitting at the finishing stage.

When using this method for working even stripes, the old yarn will be needed again further up the work, so do not cut off the old yarn. Carry it up the side of the knitting until you need it again, but take care not to pull it too tightly as this would distort your knitting.

INCREASING AND DECREASING

Several methods can be used to increase and decrease, but these are the most common:

Decreasing one stitch (K2tog) (sl1, K1, psso) (SSK) – These are all methods used to decrease the number of stitches in a row, to shape armholes and necklines. Decreases are also used in conjunction with a yarn over to create eyelets in lace patterns. Decreases are shown on page 16.

Decreasing one stitch on a purl row (P2tog) – This is the method used to decrease the number of stitches on a purl row.

Increasing one stitch (M1) - This is the method of increasing the number of stitches in a row, and is shown on page 17.

BINDING (CASTING) OFF

This is the method of securing stitches at the top of your knitted fabric. It is important that the bound off edge is elastic like the rest of your knitting, so if you find that your cast off is too tight, try using a larger needle to cast off. You can cast off knitwise or purlwise, or even in a combination of stitches, such as rib.

Casting on, Thumb Method

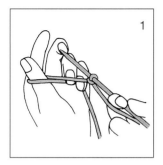

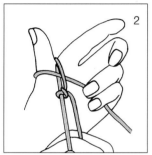

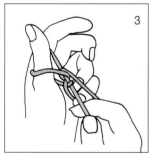

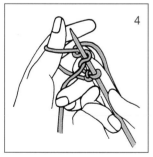

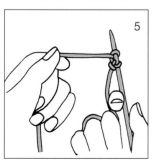

1. Make a slip knot the required length from the end of the yarn (for a practice piece make this length about 1 meter (1 yard). Place the slip knot on a needle and hold the needle in the right hand with the ball end of yarn over your first finger. Hold the other end in the palm of your left hand. Wind the loose end of the yarn around the left thumb from front to back.

2. Insert the needle upward through the yarn on the thumb.

3. Wrap the yarn over the point of the needle with your right index finger.

4. Draw the yarn back through the loop on the thumb to form a stitch.

5. Remove the yarn from your left thumb and pull the loose end to tighten the stitch. Repeat from * until the required number of stitches has been cast on.

How to Knit

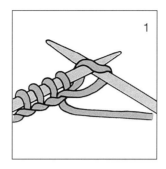

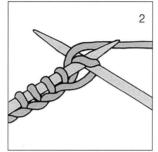

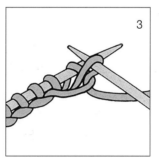

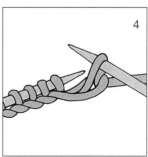

1. Hold the needle with the cast-on stitches in the left hand. With the yarn at the back of the work, insert the right-hand needle as shown through the front of the first stitch on the left-hand needle.

2. Wind the yarn from left to right over the point of the right-hand needle.

3. Draw the yarn back through the stitch, forming a loop on the right-hand needle.

4. Slip the original stitch off the left-hand needle.

To knit a row, repeat steps 1-4 until all the stitches are transferred to the right-hand needle, then turn the work, transferring the needles to work the next row.

How to Purl

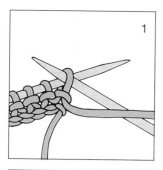

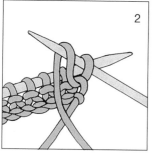

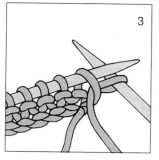

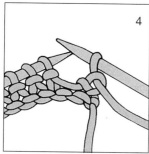

1. With the yarn at the front of the work, insert the right-hand needle as shown through the front of the first stitch on the left-hand needle.

2. Wind the yarn from right to left over the point of the right-hand needle.

3. Draw a loop through onto the right-hand needle.

4. Slip the original stitch off the left-hand needle.

To purl a row, repeat steps 1–4 until all the stitches are transferred to the right-hand needle, then turn the work, transferring the needles, to work the next row.

Decreasing

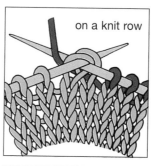

on a knit row

on a purl row

On a knit row, insert the right-hand needle from left to right through two stitches at once, then knit them together as one stitch. This is called "knit two together (k2tog)," and on the right side of the work the decrease slopes toward the right.

On a purl row insert the right-hand needle from right to left through two stitches instead of one, then purl them together as one stitch. This is called "purl two together (p2tog)." Where this is worked on a wrong side row, the decrease slopes toward the right on the right side of the work.

Decreasing – Sl1, K1, psso/K2tog tbl

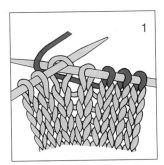

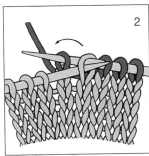

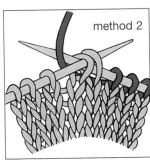

method 2

Sl1, K1, psso

1. Slip the first stitch onto the right-hand needle in a knitwise direction but without knitting it, then knit the next stitch.

2. Using the left-hand needle, lift the slipped stitch over the knitted stitch and off the needle. This is called "slip one, knit one, pass slipped stitch over (sl1, k1, psso)." Some patterns abbreviate this process as "SKP."

K2tog tbl: This is worked in a similar way to k2tog, but the stitches are knitted through the back of the loops, thus twisting the stitches. Insert the right-hand needle from right to left through the back of the first two stitches, then knit them together as one stitch. This is called "knit two together through back of loops (k2tog tbl).

Increasing One (M1)

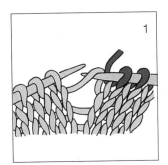

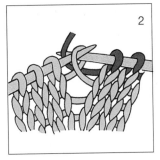

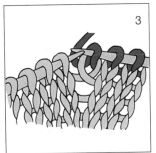

1. Insert the right-hand needle from front to back under the horizontal strand which runs between the stitches on the right and left-hand needles.

2. Insert the left-hand needle under the strand from front to back and take the right-hand needle out. Insert the right-hand needle back into the loop as shown.

3. Now knit or purl through the back of the loop to twist the new stitch so that a small hole will not form.

charts and techniques

KNITTING FROM CHARTS

Some of the knitting instructions for the patterns in this book use both written and visual instructions in the form of a chart. Once you begin to visualise your knitting as the chart, it becomes easier to be more creative, because you can treat knitting as a picture and paint with colour or texture.

Reading a chart is easier if you visualise it as the right side of a piece of knitting, working from the lower edge to the top. Each square on the chart represents one stitch; each line of squares indicates a row of knitting. When working from the chart, read odd numbered rows – 1, 3, 5 (right side of fabric) – from right to left and even numbered rows – 2, 4, 6 (wrong side of fabric) – from left to right.

In this book, charts form part of the instructions for patterns with lace, Fair Isle, cable, or textured designs, or where a combination of techniques is used. Along with the chart you will also find a key, which explains the symbols used to create the pattern.

KNITTING WITH COLOUR

Fair Isle – Fair Isle is the term used for multi-coloured stocking stitch patterns, where two or more colours are used across a single row of knitting. This method of knitting involves carrying the colour not in use loosely across the wrong side of the work. If the strands have to be carried over more than four stitches there is a danger that they could be pulled when the garment is put on or pulled off. To avoid this, twist together the yarn being used with the yarn not being used every third stitch. When working the Fair Isle technique it is essential that you are aware of your tension. The yarn at the back must be stranded very loosely to maintain the elasticity of the fabric.

If you are learning this as a new technique, it is a good idea to practice the pattern on waste yarn first to become familiar with this method of knitting. The Fair Isle design in this book uses a chart for the colour pattern. Each separate colour used is given a letter in the pattern, which corresponds with a symbol on the chart.

KNITTING WITH TEXTURE

Lace – The lace patterns in this book are achieved by using the eyelet method of increasing. This is usually worked along with a decrease, so the number of stitches remains constant at the end of each row. In a chart, the key explains the combination of stitches needed to achieve the design. Lace patterns can be quite complex to work and require concentration to become familiar with the pattern, but the effect is very rewarding.

Basic cables – Cables are created where one set of stitches is held at the back or front of the work on a separate needle, while the following group is knitted, giving a crossover twisted effect, either to the right or left.

Twisting stitches – These involve two or more stitches traveling across the fabric in a diagonal direction. Altering the direction of a group of stitches requires a "twisting" technique using a cable needle. For example, two stitches in stocking stitch are moved across a reverse stocking stitch background by crossing them successively over one purl stitch on alternate rows. The number of stitches in a twist can vary according to the pattern being worked. In a chart, the key will explain the combination of stitches needed to achieve the design.

Texture – This is a simple technique that invloves using a combination of knit and purl stitches to create a relief pattern. This can be an all over pattern or create a motif, such as textured hearts. We have used charts for some of these designs. A symbol on the chart indicates the change between knit and purl stitches.

finishing

FINISHING YOUR WORK

After spending many hours knitting it is essential that you take some time to complete your project correctly. These instructions show you just how easy it is to achieve a beautifully finished knitted garment.

PRESSING AND BLOCKING

With the wrong side of the fabric facing up, pin out each knitted piece onto an ironing board, matching all the measurements given in the pattern. As each yarn is different, refer to the ball band and press the pieces according to the instructions given. Pressing the knitted fabric will help the pieces maintain their shape and give a smooth finish.

SEWING IN ENDS

Once you have pressed your finished pieces, sew in all loose ends. Thread a darning needle with yarn, weave the needle through approximately five stitches on the wrong side of the fabric, then pull the yarn through. Then weave the needle in the opposite direction for approximately five stitches and pull the yarn through again. Cut the end of the yarn. Do not pull the woven yarn tight or the knitted fabric may pucker up.

Many knitters find this a very tedious task, but it is well worth the effort. Sew in all ends – do not be tempted to use a long yarn end for sewing a seam! Always use a separate length of yarn for sewing up, because if you make a mistake you can undo the stitches without any danger of unravelling part of your knitting.

SEWING SEAMS

There are two main stitches that are used for sewing up seams:

Mattress stitch – This method of sewing up is worked on the right side of the fabric and is ideal for matching stripes. Mattress stitch should be worked one knitted stitch in from the edge to give the best finish.

Secure the end of the sewing yarn on the wrong side, at the bottom of one of the edges to be joined. With the right side of the work facing, lay the two pieces to be joined edge to edge. Insert the needle from the wrong side between the first (or edge) stitch and the second stitch and pull the yarn through. *Take the needle across to the same place on the opposite piece, insert it from the front, and pass it under the loops between the first and second stitches on the next two rows. Bring the needle back through to the front and take it back across to the first piece of knitted fabric. Insert the needle back through where it came out, and under the loops between stitches on the next two rows. Pull the yarn through to join the two pieces. Repeat from * to sew up the whole seam.

Back stitch – Pin the pieces with right sides together. Insert the needle into the fabric at the end, one stitch or row in from the edge, then take the needle around the two edges to secure them. Insert the needle into the fabric just behind where the last stitch came out and make a short stitch. Re-insert the needle where the previous stitch started, then bring the needle up to make a longer stitch. Next, re-insert needle where last stitch ended. Repeat to the end of the seam, taking care to match any patterning.

double
knitting

fitted sweater

This simple silhouette forms the foundation for three designs. Whether it be a polo neck, V-neck or short-sleeved version, each offers plenty of versatility.

To fit bust size:					
81	86	91	97	102	107 cm
32	**34**	**36**	**38**	**40**	**42 in.**

Actual width at underarm (A):

85	91	96	102	107	111 cm
33^1/$_2$	35^3/$_4$	38	40	42	43^3/$_4$ in.

Finished length (B):

52	53	54	55	56	57 cm
20^1/$_2$	21	21^1/$_4$	21^3/$_4$	22	22^1/$_2$ in.

Long-sleeve length to underarm (C):

44	45	45	45	46	46 cm
17^1/$_4$	17^3/$_4$	17^3/$_4$	17^3/$_4$	18	18 in.

^{3}/$_4$-sleeve length to underarm (C):

36	36	38	38	40	40 cm
14^1/$_4$	14^1/$_4$	15	15	15^3/$_4$	15^3/$_4$ in.

Short-sleeve length to underarm (C):

5	5	6	6	7	7 cm
2	2	2^1/$_4$	2^1/$_4$	2^3/$_4$	2^3/$_4$ in.

YARN

Poloneck version
50g balls of Impression (Kid Mohair/Polyamide), #5 Blue Mix:

7	7	8	8	9	9

V-neck version
25g balls of Kimono Angora (Angora/wool/nylon), #2 Blue Mix:

7	7	8	8	9	9

Short-sleeved scoop-neck version
50g balls of Kashmir DK (Merino/cashmere/microfiber), #2 Blue

7	7	8	8	9	9

NEEDLES

Pair of 3^1/$_4$ mm (US 3) knitting needles
Pair of 4 mm (US 6) knitting needles

TENSION

22 sts and 30 rows = 10 cm (4in.) square measured over st st using 4 mm (US 6) knitting needles.

Poloneck version

BACK

Using 3^1/$_4$ mm (US 3) needles, cast on 94 (102, 114, 118, 122) sts.

Rib row 1: [K2, P2] 23 (25, 26, 28, 29, 30) times, K2.
Rib row 2: [P2, K2] 23 (25, 26, 28, 29, 30) times, P2.
These 2 rows form rib.
Work in rib for a further 18 rows, dec 0 (1, 0, 1, 0, 0) sts at each end of last row, ending with WS row: 94 (100, 106, 112, 118, 122) sts.
Change to 4 mm (US 6) needles.
Work 2 rows st st, ending with WS row.
**Next row (RS) (dec): K3, K2tog, knit to last 5 sts, K2tog tbl, K3.
Working all decs as set by last row, cont in st st, dec 1 st at each end of every 6th row until there are 84 (90, 96, 102, 108, 112) sts.
Cont to work even until work measures 21 (22, 22, 23, 23, 24) cm [8^1/$_4$ (8^1/$_2$, 8^1/$_2$, 9, 9, 9^1/$_2$) in.] ending with WS row.
Next row (RS) (inc): K3, M1, knit to last 3 sts, M1, K3.
Working all incs as set by last row, cont in st st, inc 1 st at each end of every 6th row until there are 94 (100, 106, 112, 118, 122) sts.
Cont to work even until work measures 34 (35, 35, 36, 36, 37) cm [13^1/$_4$ (13^3/$_4$, 13^3/$_4$, 14^1/$_4$, 14^1/$_4$, 14^1/$_2$) in.], ending with WS row.
Shape armholes
Cast off 4 (5, 5, 6, 6, 6) sts at beg next 2 rows, and 3 (3, 3, 4, 4, 4) sts at beg foll 2 rows: 80 (84, 90, 92, 98, 102) sts.
Next row (RS) (dec): K3, K2tog, knit to last 5 sts, K2tog tbl, K3.
Next row (WS) (dec): P3, P2tog tbl, purl to last 5 sts, P2tog, P3.
Next row (RS) (dec): K3, K2tog, knit to last 5 sts, K2tog tbl, K3.
Working all decs as set by last row, dec 1 st at each end of every other row until 72 (74, 76, 78, 82, 86) sts rem.

Poloneck version

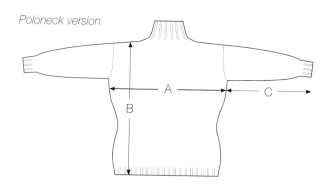

V-neck version

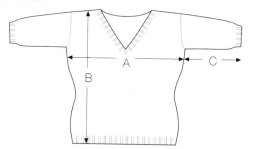

Short-sleeved version

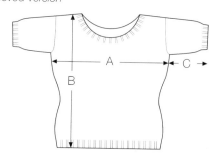

Cont working even until armhole measures 18 (18, 19, 19, 20, 20) cm [7 (7, 7½, 7½, 8, 8) in.], ending with WS row.

Shape shoulders and back neck

Cast off 7 (7, 7, 8, 8, 9) sts at beg next 2 rows: 58 (60, 62, 62, 66, 68) sts.

Cast off 7 (7, 7, 8, 8, 9) sts, knit until there are 9 (10, 11, 10, 12, 12) sts on RH needle and turn, place rem sts on a holder. Work both sides of neck separately.

Cast off 3 sts, purl to end.

Cast off rem 6 (7, 8, 7, 9, 9) sts.

With RS facing, rejoin yarn to sts from holder, cast off centre 26 sts, knit to end.

Complete to match first side, reversing shaping and working an extra row before start of shoulder shaping.

FRONT

Work as given for back until you have worked16 rows less than on back to start of shoulder shaping, ending with WS row.

Shape front neck

Next row (RS): K30 (31, 32, 33, 35, 37) and turn, place rem sts on a holder.

Next row: Cast off 4 sts, purl to end: 26 (27, 28, 29, 31, 33) sts.

Dec 1 st at neck edge on next 3 rows, then every other row twice, then on foll 4th row: 20 (21, 22, 23, 25, 27) sts.

Work 3 rows, ending with WS row.

Shape shoulder

Next row (RS): Cast off 7 (7, 7, 8, 8, 9) sts at beg of row and on next RS row.

Work 1 row even.

Cast off rem 6 (7, 8, 7, 9, 9) sts.

With RS facing, rejoin yarn to rem sts, cast off centre 12 sts, knit to end.

Complete to match first side, reversing shapings and working an extra row before start of shoulder shaping.

SLEEVES (work both the same)

Using 3¹/₄ mm (US 3) needles, cast on 56 (56, 58, 58, 60, 60) sts.

Rib row 1: P1 (1, 0, 0, 1, 1), (K2, P2) 13 (13, 14, 14, 14, 14) times, K2, P1 (1, 0, 0, 1, 1).

Rib row 2: K1 (1, 0, 0, 1, 1), (P2, K2) 13 (13, 14, 14, 14, 14) times, P2, K1 (1, 0, 0, 1, 1). These 2 rows form rib.

Work in rib for a further 18 rows, inc 1 st at each end of 13th of these rows, and ending with WS row: 58 (58, 60, 60, 62, 62) sts.

Change to 4 mm (US 6) needles.

Next row (RS): Beg st st and work 10 rows, ending with WS row.

Next row (RS) (inc): K3, M1, knit to last 3 sts, M1, K3.

Working all incs as set by last row, cont in st st, inc 1 st at each end of every 14th (14th, 14th, 14th, 12th, 12th) row to 72 (72, 64, 64, 70, 70) sts, then on every foll 0 (0, 12th, 12th, 10th, 10th) row until there are 72 (72, 76, 76, 80, 80) sts.

Work even until sleeve measures 44 (45, 45, 45, 46, 46) cm [7¹/₄ (17³/₄, 17³/₄, 17³/₄, 18, 18) in.], ending with WS row.

Shape sleevehead

***Cast off 5 sts at beg next 2 rows, and 3 sts at beg foll 2 rows:

56 (56, 60, 60, 64, 64) sts.

Dec 1 st at each end of next 3 rows and the every other row 3 times: 44 (44, 48, 48, 52, 52) sts.

Work 3 rows even.

Dec 1 st at each end of next row and then every 4th row 3 times: 36 (36, 40, 40, 44, 44) sts.

Work 1 row even.

Dec 1 st at each end of next row and then every other row twice, then on every row to 24 (24, 28, 28, 32, 32) sts.

Cast off 3 sts at beg of next 4 rows.

Cast off rem 12 (12, 16, 16, 20, 20) sts.

FINISHING

Press as described on page 21.

Join right shoulder seam.

Collar

With RS facing and using 3¹/₄ mm (US 3) needles, pick up and knit 25 sts down left front neck, 14 sts across centre front, 25 sts up right front neck, and 42 sts across back neck: 106 sts.

Rib row 1: (K2, P2) to last 2 sts, K2.

Rib row 2: (P2, K2) to last 2 sts, P2.

These 2 rows form rib.

Work until rib measures 10cm (4 in).

Cast off in rib.

Join left shoulder and collar seam.

Join side and sleeve seams.

Place centre of Cast off edge to shoulder seam, set in sleeve, easing sleevehead into armhole.

V-neck version

BACK

Using 3¹/₄ mm (US 3) needles, cast on 94 (100, 106, 112, 118, 122) sts.

Row 1: *K1, P1, rep from * to end.

Row 2: *P1, K1, rep from * to end.

These 2 rows form moss stitch.

Work in moss stitch for a further 4 rows, ending with WS row.

Change to 4 mm (US 6) needles.

On next RS row, beg st st and work for 16 rows.

Complete as given for back of poloneck version from **.

FRONT

Work as given for back to beg of armhole shaping, ending with WS row.

Shape armholes

Cast off 4 (5, 5, 6, 6, 6) sts at beg next 2 rows: 86 (90, 96, 100, 106, 110) sts.

Shape front neck

Next row (RS): Cast off 3 (3, 3, 4, 4, 4) sts, knit until there are 38 (40, 43, 44, 47, 49) sts on right needle, K2tog tbl and turn, place rem sts on a holder.

Work 1 row even.

Working all neck shaping decs as set and armhole decs as given for back, dec 1 st at armhole edge of next 3 rows and 1 (2, 4, 4, 5, 5) alt rows, and at the same time, dec 1 st at neck edge on next every other row: 32 (32, 31, 32, 33, 35) sts.

Cont to dec at neck edge only every other row for 4 (3, 1, 1, 0, 0) times, then on every foll 4th row until 20 (21, 22, 23, 25, 27) sts rem. Work even until front matches back to start of shoulder shaping, ending with WS row.

Shape shoulder

Next row (RS): Cast off 7 (7, 7, 8, 8, 9) sts at beg of row and on next RS row.

Work 1 row even.

Cast off rem 6 (7, 8, 7, 9, 9) sts.

With RS facing, rejoin yarn to rem sts, K2tog, knit to end.

Complete to match first side, reversing shaping and working an extra row before start of shoulder shaping.

SLEEVES (work both the same)

Using 3¼ mm (US 3) needles, cast on 58 (58, 60, 60, 62, 62) sts.

Row 1: *K1, P1, rep from * to end.

Row 2: *P1, K1, rep from * to end.

These 2 rows form moss stitch.

Work in moss stitch for a further 4 rows, ending with WS row.

Change to 4 mm (US 6) needles.

Next row (RS): Work in st st for 8 rows.

Next row (RS) (inc): K3, M1, knit to last 3 sts, M1, K3.

Working all incs as set by last row, cont in st st, inc 1 st at each end of every foll 12th row until there are 72 (72, 76, 76, 80, 80) sts.

Work even until sleeve measures 36 (36, 38, 38, 40, 40) cm

[14¼ (14¼, 15, 15, 15¾, 15¾) in.], ending with WS row.

Shape sleevehead

Complete as given for sleeve of poloneck version from ***.

FINISHING

Press as described on page 21.

Join right shoulder seam.

Neckband

With RS facing and using 3¼ mm (US 3) needles, pick up and knit 47 (47, 49, 49, 51, 51) sts down left front neck, 1 st from centre front and mark this st, 47 (47, 49, 49, 51, 51) sts up right front neck, and 32 sts across back neck: 127 (127, 131, 131, 135, 135) sts.

Next row (WS): *K1, P1, rep from * to last st, K1.

This row sets moss st.

Cont in moss st as folls:

Next row (RS) (dec): Work in patt to within 1 st of marked st, sl1, K2tog, psso, patt to end.

Rep last 2 rows once more.

Cast off knitwise on WS, dec 2 sts at centre front as before.

Join left shoulder and neckband seam.

Join side and sleeve seams.

Match centre of Cast off edge to shoulder seam, set in sleeve, easing sleevehead into armhole.

Short-sleeved scoop-neck version

BACK

Using 3¼ mm (US 3) needles, cast on 94 (100, 106, 112, 118, 122) sts and work 6 rows in garter st, ending with WS row.

Change to 4 mm (US 6) needles.

Beg with a knit row, work in st st for 16 rows, ending with WS row.

Work as given for back of poloneck version until armhole measures 17 (17, 18, 18, 19, 19) cm [14¼ (14¼, 15, 15, 15¾, 15¾) in.], ending with WS row.

Shape back neck

right: V-neck version

Next row (RS): K23 (24, 25, 26, 28, 30) and turn, place rem sts on a holder.

Next row: Cast off 6 sts, purl to end: 17 (18, 19, 20, 22, 24) sts.

Dec 1 st at neck edge on next 2 rows, ending with WS row.

Shape shoulder

Cast off 6 (7, 7, 8, 9, 10) sts and dec 1 st at end of next row.

Dec 1 st at beg of next row.

Cast off rem 7 (7, 8, 8, 9, 10) sts.

With RS facing, rejoin yarn to rem sts, cast off centre 26 sts, knit to end.

Complete to match first side, reversing shaping and working an extra row before start of shoulder shaping.

FRONT

Work as given for back until you have worked 24 rows less than on back to start of shoulder shaping, ending with RS facing for next row.

Shape front neck

Next row (RS): K27 (28, 29, 30, 32, 34) and turn, place rem sts on a holder.

Next row: Cast off 6 sts, purl to end: 21 (22, 23, 24, 26, 28) sts.

Dec 1 st at neck edge on next 3 rows, then every other row 3 times, then on every foll 4th row until 13 (14, 15, 16, 18, 20) sts rem.

Work 5 rows, ending with WS row.

Shape shoulder

Next row (RS): Cast off 6 (7, 7, 8, 9, 10) sts at beg of row.

Work 1 row even.

Cast off rem 7 (7, 8, 8, 9, 10) sts.

With RS facing, rejoin yarn to rem sts, cast off centre 14 sts, knit to end.

Complete to match first side, reversing shaping and working an extra row before start of shoulder shaping.

SLEEVES (work both the same)

Using 3¼ mm (US 3) needles, cast on 68 (68, 72, 72, 76, 76) sts and work 6 rows in garter st, ending with WS row.

Change to 4 mm (US 6) needles.

Beg with a K row, work in st st, inc 1 st at each end of next row and foll 4th row: 72 (72, 76, 76, 80, 80) sts.

Work even until sleeve measures 5 (5, 6, 6, 7, 7) cm [2 (2, 2¼, 2¼, 2¾, 2¾) in], ending with WS row.

Shape sleevehead

Complete as given for sleeve of poloneck version from ***.

FINISHING

Press as described on page 21.

Join right shoulder.

K4 rows.

Join left shoulder and neckband seam.

Join side and sleeve seams.

Place centre of cast-off edge to shoulder, set in sleeve, easing in fullness.

Neckband

With RS facing and using 3¼ mm (US 3) needles, pick up and knit 27 sts down left front neck, 14 sts across centre front, 27 sts up right front neck, and 40 sts across back neck: 108 sts.

Knit 4 rows.

Cast off knitwise on WS.

Join left shoulder and neckband seam.

Join side and sleeve seams.

Match centre of cast off edge to shoulder seam. Set in sleeve, easing sleevehead into armhole.

right: short-sleeved scoop-neck version

basic sweater

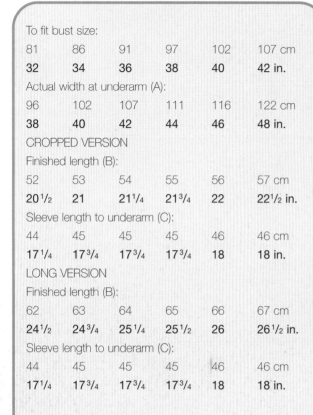

To fit bust size:

81	86	91	97	102	107 cm
32	**34**	**36**	**38**	**40**	**42 in.**

Actual width at underarm (A):

96	102	107	111	116	122 cm
38	**40**	**42**	**44**	**46**	**48 in.**

CROPPED VERSION
Finished length (B):

52	53	54	55	56	57 cm
20½	**21**	**21¼**	**21¾**	**22**	**22½ in.**

Sleeve length to underarm (C):

44	45	45	45	46	46 cm
17¼	**17¾**	**17¾**	**17¾**	**18**	**18 in.**

LONG VERSION
Finished length (B):

62	63	64	65	66	67 cm
24½	**24¾**	**25¼**	**25½**	**26**	**26½ in.**

Sleeve length to underarm (C):

44	45	45	45	46	46 cm
17¼	**17¾**	**17¾**	**17¾**	**18**	**18 in.**

YARN
Cropped version
50g balls of Kashmir DK (Merino/cashmere/microfiber),
#1 Cream:

10	10	11	11	12	12

Long version
25g balls of Kimono Angora (Angora/wool/nylon),#3 Brown

9	9	10	10	11	11

NEEDLES
Pair of 3¾ mm (US 5) knitting needles
Pair of 4 mm (US 6) knitting needles

TENSION
22 sts and 30 rows = 10 cm (4 in.) square measured over
st st using 4 mm (US 6) knitting needles.

This simple sweater can be easily adapted to look quite different. The patterns are for either full-length or cropped versions, with two alternative necklines.

BACK

Using 3¾ mm (US 5) needles, cast on 106 (112, 118, 122, 128, 134) sts.

Rib row 1: K1 (4, 1, 3, 0, 3), *P2, K4, rep from * to last 3 (6, 3, 5, 2, 5) sts, P2, K1 (4, 1, 3, 0, 3).

Rib row 2: P1 (4, 1, 3, 0, 3), *K2, P4, rep from * to last 3 (6, 3, 5, 2, 5) sts, K2, P1 (4, 1, 3, 0, 3).

These 2 rows form rib.

Work in rib for further 18 rows, end with WS row.

Change to 4 mm (US 6) needles.

Cropped version only:

Beg with a knit row, work in st st until work measures 33 (34, 34, 35, 35, 36) cm [13 (13½, 13½, 13¾, 13¾, 14¼) in.], end with RS facing for next row.

Full-length version only:

Beg with a knit row, work in st st until work measures 43 (44, 44, 45, 45, 46) cm [17 (17¼, 17¼, 17¾, 17¾, 18) in.], ending with WS row.

Shape armholes (both versions):

Cast off 6 sts at beg next 2 rows, and 4 sts at beg foll 2 rows: 86 (92, 98, 102, 108, 114) sts.

Dec 1 st at each end of next 3 rows and then for 2 (2, 3, 3, 4, 5) times: 76 (82, 86, 90, 94, 98) sts.

Work 3 rows even.

Dec 1 st at each end of next row: 74 (80, 84, 88, 92, 96) sts.

Work even until armhole measures 19 (19, 20, 20, 21, 21) cm [7½ (7½, 8, 8, 8¼, 8¼) in.], ending with WS row.

Shape shoulders and back neck

Cast off 6 (7, 8, 8, 9, 10) sts at beg next 2 rows: 62 (66, 68, 72, 74, 76) sts.

Cast off 6 (7, 8, 8, 9, 10) sts, knit until there are 9 (10, 10, 12, 12, 12) sts on RH needle and turn, place rem sts on a holder.

Work both sides of neck separately.

Cast off 3 sts, purl to end.

Cast off rem 6 (7, 7, 9, 9, 9) sts.

With RS facing rejoin yarn to sts from holder, cast off centre 32 sts, knit to end.

Complete to match first side, reversing shapings and working an extra row before start of shoulder shaping.

FRONT

Work as given for back until you have worked 18 rows fewer than on back to start of shoulder shaping, ending with RS facing for next row.

Shape front neck

Next row (RS): K29 (32, 34, 36, 38, 40) and turn, place rem sts on a holder.

Next row: Cast off 4 sts, purl to end: 25 (28, 30, 32, 34, 36) sts. Dec 1 st at neck edge on next 4 rows and then every other row 4 times: 18 (21, 23, 25, 27, 29) sts.

Work 6 rows, ending with RS facing for next row.

Shape shoulder

Cast off 6 (7, 8, 8, 9, 10) sts at beg next 2 RS rows.

Work 1 row even.

Cast off rem 6 (7, 7, 9, 9, 9) sts.

With RS facing rejoin yarn to rem sts, cast off centre 16 sts, knit to end.

Complete to match first side, reversing shaping and working an extra row before start of shoulder shaping.

Long version

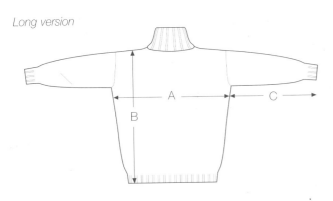

Cropped version

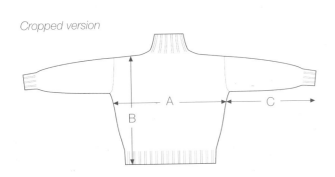

SLEEVES (work both the same)

Using 3¾ mm (US 5) needles, cast on 54 (54, 56, 56, 58, 58) sts.

Cropped version only:

Rib row 1: K2 (2, 3, 3, 4, 4), *P2, K4, rep from * to last 4 (4, 5, 5, 6, 6) sts, P2, K2 (2, 3, 3, 4, 4).

Rib row 2: P2 (2, 3, 3, 4, 4), *K2, P4, rep from * to last 4 (4, 5, 5, 6, 6) sts, K2, P2 (2, 3, 3, 4, 4).

These 2 rows form rib.

Work in rib for a further 18 rows, inc 1 st at each end of 13th of these rows, and ending with WS row: 58 (58, 60, 60, 62, 62) sts.

Full-length version only:

Rib row 1: P2 (2, 3, 3, 4, 4), *K2, P4, rep from * to last 4 (4, 5, 5, 6, 6) sts, K2, P2 (2, 3, 3, 4, 4).

Rib row 2: K2 (2, 3, 3, 4, 4), *P2, K4, rep from * to last 4 (4, 5, 5, 6, 6) sts, P2, K2 (2, 3, 3, 4, 4).

These 2 rows form rib.

Work in rib for a further 38 rows, inc 1 st at each end of 13th and 33rd of these rows, and ending with WS row: 56 (56, 58, 58, 60, 60) sts.

Both versions:

Change to 4 mm (US 6) needles.

Beg with a knit row, work in st st as folls:

Work 4 (4, 4, 4, 6, 6) rows, ending with WS row.

Inc 1 st at each end of next row and every foll 10th row until there are 74 (74, 76, 76, 78, 78) sts.

Work even until sleeve measures 44 (45, 45, 45, 46, 46) cm [17¼ (17¾, 17¾, 17¾, 18, 18) in.], ending with WS row.

Shape sleevehead

Cast off 5 sts at beg of next 2 rows, and then cast off 3 sts at beg of foll 2 rows: 58 (58, 60, 60, 62, 62) sts.

Dec 1 st at each end of next 3 rows and then 1 st each end of every other row 3 times: 46 (46, 48, 48, 50, 50) sts.

Work 3 rows even.

Dec 1 st at each end of next row and foll 4th row twice: 40 (40, 42, 42, 44, 44) sts.

Work 1 row even.

Dec 1 st at each end of next row and then every other row 3 (3, 4, 4, 5, 5) times, then on 3 foll rows: 26 (26, 26, 26, 26, 26) sts.

Cast off 3 sts at beg next 4 rows.

Cast off rem 14 sts.

FINISHING

Press as described on page 21.

Join right shoulder seam.

Make collar

With RS facing and using 3¾ mm (US 5) needles, pick up and knit and knit 23 sts down left front neck, 16 sts across centre front, 23 sts up right front neck, and 38 sts across back neck: 100 sts.

Cropped version:

Rib row 1: [K2, P4] to last 2 sts, K2.

Rib row 2: [P2, K4] to last 2 sts, P2.

These 2 rows form rib.

Work until rib measures 8 cm (3 in.).

Cast off in rib.

Full-length version:

Rib row 1: [P2, K4] to last 2 sts, P2.

Rib row 2: [K2, P4] to last 2 sts, K2.

These 2 rows form rib.

Work until rib measures 20 cm (8 in.).

Cast off in rib.

Both versions:

Join left shoulder and collar seam, reversing seam for turn-back on full-length sweater collar.

Join side and sleeve seams.

Match centre of cast off edge to shoulder seam.

Set in sleeve, easing sleevehead into armhole.

V-neck cardigan

Every woman needs at least one V-neck cardigan in her wardrobe, and this stylish design can be knitted either plain or in a pretty lace pattern.

Simple version

BACK

Using US 3 (3¼ mm) needles, cast on 101 (107, 113, 117, 123, 129) sts and knit 4 rows, ending with WS row.

Change to 4 mm (US 6) needles and beg with a knit row, work in st st until work measures 31 (31, 32, 32, 33, 33) cm [12¼ (12¼, 12½, 12½, 13, 13) in.], ending with WS row.

**Shape armholes

Cast off 5 (5, 6, 6, 6, 7) sts at beg next 2 rows, and 3 (3, 3, 4, 4, 4) sts at beg foll 2 rows: 85 (91, 95, 97, 103, 107) sts.

Dec 1 st at each end of next 3 (5, 5, 5, 7, 7) rows, then on every other row until 77 (79, 81, 83, 85, 87) sts rem.

Work even until armhole measures 19 (20, 20, 21, 21, 22) cm [7½ (8, 8, 8¼, 8¼, 8¾) in.], ending with WS row.

Shape shoulders and back neck

Cast off 7 (7, 7, 7, 7, 8) sts at beg next 2 rows: 63 (65, 67, 69, 71, 71) sts.

Cast off 7 (7, 7, 7, 7, 8) sts, work in patt until there are 10 (11, 11, 12, 12, 11) sts on RH needle and turn, place rem sts on a holder.

Work both sides of neck separately.

Cast off 4 sts, purl to end.

Cast off rem 6 (7, 7, 8, 8, 7) sts.

With RS facing, rejoin yarn to sts from holder and cast off centre 29 (29, 31, 31, 33, 33) sts, work in patt to end.

Complete to match first side, reversing shaping and working an extra row before start of shoulder shaping.

LEFT FRONT

Using US 3 (3¼ mm) needles, cast on 52 (55, 58, 60, 63, 66) sts and knit 4 rows, ending with WS row.

Change to 4 mm (US 6) needles and beg with a knit row, work

To fit bust size:

81	86	91	97	102	107 cm
32	**34**	**36**	**38**	**40**	**42 in.**

Actual width at underarm (A):

92	97	103	106	112	117 cm
36¼	**38¼**	**40½**	**41¾**	**44**	**46 in.**

Finished length (B):

50	51	52	53	54	55 cm
19½	**20**	**20½**	**21**	**21¼**	**21¾ in.**

Sleeve length to underarm (C):

45	45	45	46	46	46 cm
17¾	**17¾**	**17¾**	**18**	**18**	**18 in.**

YARN

Simple version
50g balls of Kashmir DK (Merino/cashmere/microfiber), #4 Rose:

10	10	11	11	12	12

Lace version
50g balls of Impression (Kid/mohair/polyamide), #6 Lilac Mix:

7	7	8	8	9	9

NEEDLES
Pair of 3¼ mm (US 3) knitting needles
Pair of 4 mm (US 6) knitting needles
3¼ mm (US 3) circular needle

BUTTONS
7 small pearl buttons

TENSION
22 sts and 30 rows = 10 cm (4 in) square measured over st st using 4 mm (US 6) knitting needles.

in st st until left front matches back to beg of armhole shaping, ending with WS row.

**Shape armhole and front neck*

Cast off 5 (5, 6, 6, 6, 7) sts at beg and dec 1 st at end of next row. Work 1 row even.

Cast off 3 (3, 3, 4, 4, 4) sts at beg and dec 1 st at end of next row: 42 (45, 47, 48, 51, 53) sts.

Dec 1 st at armhole edge of next 3 (5, 5, 5, 7, 7) rows, then on every other row 1 (1, 2, 2, 2, 3) times and at the same time, dec 1 st at neck edge on next row and then every other row: 35 (35, 35, 36, 36, 36) sts.

Work 1 row, ending with WS row.

Dec 1 st at neck edge only on next row and every other row until 20 (21, 21, 22, 22, 23) sts rem.

Work even until left front matches back to start of shoulder shaping, ending with WS row.

Shape shoulder

Cast off 7 (7, 7, 7, 7, 8) sts at beg next 2 RS rows.

Work 1 row even.

Cast off rem 6 (7, 7, 8, 8, 7) sts.

RIGHT FRONT

Using 3 1/4 mm (US 3) needles, cast on 52 (55, 58, 60, 63, 66) sts and knit 4 rows, ending with WS row.

Change to 4 mm (US 6) needles and beg with a knit row, work in st st, complete to match left front, reversing shaping and working an extra row before start of armhole, neck and shoulder shaping.

SLEEVES (work both the same)

Using 3 1/4 mm (US 3) needles, cast on 53 (53, 55, 55, 57, 57) sts and knit 4 rows, ending with WS row.

Change to 4 mm (US 6) needles and beg with a knit row, work in st st, inc 1 st at each end of 13th row and every foll 10th row until there are 77 (77, 79, 79, 81, 81) sts.

**Work even until sleeve measures 45 (45, 45, 46, 46, 46) cm [7 3/4 (17 3/4, 17 3/4, 18, 18, 18) in], ending with WS row.

Shape sleevehead

Cast off 5 (5, 6, 6, 6, 7) sts at beg next 2 rows, and 3 (3, 3, 4, 4, 4) sts at beg foll 2 rows: 61 (61, 61, 59, 61, 59) sts.

Dec 1 st at each end of next 3 rows, then dec 1 st every other row 2 (2, 2, 1, 1, 0) times, then on every foll 4th row until 41 (39, 39, 37, 39, 37) sts rem.

Work 1 row even.

Dec 1 st at each end of next row 3 (2, 2, 2, 2, 2) RS rows.

Next row (WS): Dec 1 st at each end.

Cast off 6 sts at beg of next 2 rows.

Cast off rem 21 (21, 21, 19, 21, 19) sts.

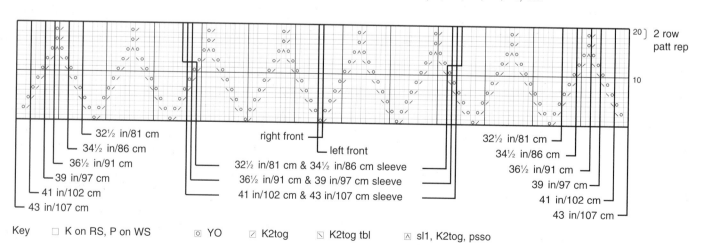

20] 2 row patt rep

10

└ 32½ in/81 cm
└ 34½ in/86 cm
└ 36½ in/91 cm
└ 39 in/97 cm
└ 41 in/102 cm
└ 43 in/107 cm

right front ─
└ left front

32½ in/81 cm & 34½ in/86 cm sleeve
36½ in/91 cm & 39 in/97 cm sleeve
41 in/102 cm & 43 in/107 cm sleeve

32½ in/81 cm
34½ in/86 cm
36½ in/91 cm
39 in/97 cm
41 in/102 cm
43 in/107 cm

Key   ☐ K on RS, P on WS   ◉ YO   ⊘ K2tog   ◺ K2tog tbl   ◮ sl1, K2tog, psso

right: lace version

Lace version

BACK

Using 3¼ mm (US 3) needles, cast on 101 (107, 113, 117, 123, 129) sts and knit 4 rows, ending with WS row.

Change to 4 mm (US 6) needles and beg with a RS row, work in patt from chart, working rows 1 to 18 once and then repeating rows 19 and 20 throughout.

Work even until work measures 31 (31, 32, 32, 33, 33) cm [12¼ (12¼, 12½, 12½, 13, 13) in.], ending with WS row.

Complete as given for back of simple version from **.

LEFT FRONT

Using 3¼ mm (US 3) needles, cast on 52 (55, 58, 60, 63, 66) sts and knit 4 rows, ending with WS row.

Change to 4 mm (US 6) needles and beg with a RS row, work in patt from chart on page 40 until left front matches back to beg of armhole shaping, ending with WS row.

Complete as given for left front of simple version from **.

RIGHT FRONT

Using 3¼ mm (US 3) needles, cast on 52 (55, 58, 60, 63, 66) sts and knit 4 rows, ending with WS row.

Change to 4 mm (US 6) needles and beg with a RS row, work in patt from chart, complete to match left front, following chart for right front and reversing shaping, working an extra row before start of armhole, neck and shoulder shaping.

SLEEVES (work both the same)

Using 3¼ mm (US 3) needles, cast on 53 (53, 55, 55, 57, 57) sts and knit 4 rows, ending with WS row.

Change to US 6 (4 mm) needles and, beg with a RS row, work in patt from chart, working rows 1 to 18 once and then repeating rows 19 and 20 throughout, and at the same time, inc 1 st at each end of chart row 13 and every foll 10th row until there are 77 (77, 79, 79, 81, 81) sts, working inc sts in patt.

Complete as given for sleeve of simple version from **.

FINISHING

Both versions:

Press as described on page 21.

Join both shoulder seams.

Make button border

With RS facing and using 3¼ mm (US 3) circular needle, starting at right front cast-on edge, pick up and knit 69 (69, 71, 71, 73, 73) sts up right front opening edge to start of neck shaping, 53 (55, 55, 57, 57, 59) sts up right front neck, 37 (37, 39, 39, 41, 41) sts from back, 53 (55, 55, 57, 57, 59) sts down left front neck, then 69 (69, 71, 71, 73, 73) sts down left front to cast-on edge: 281 (285, 291, 295, 301, 305) sts.

Knit 1 row.

Next row (buttonhole row) (RS): K1 (1, 3, 3, 5, 5), [K2tog, YO, K9] 7 times, knit to end.

Cast off knitwise on WS.

Join side and sleeve seams.

Match centre of cast-off edge to shoulder seam.

Set in sleeve, easing sleevehead into armhole.

Sew on buttons to correspond with buttonholes.

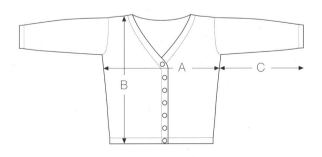

lace cardigan

To fit bust size:					
81	86	91	97	102	107 cm
32	**34**	**36**	**38**	**40**	**42 in.**
Actual width at underarm (A):					
94	98	104	108	114	118 cm
37	**38**1/2	**41**	**42**1/2	**45**	**46**1/2 **in.**
Finished length (B):					
47	48	49	50	51	52 cm
181/2	**19**	**19**1/2	**19**1/2	**20**	**20**1/2 **in.**
Sleeve length to underarm (C):					
46	46	47	47	47	48 cm
18	**18**	**18**1/2	**18**1/2	**18**1/2	**19 in.**

YARN

25g balls of Angora (Angora), #4 Berry:

6	6	7	7	7	8

NEEDLES

Pair of 3 1/4 mm (US 3) knitting needles
Pair of 4 mm (US 6) knitting needles

BUTTONS

7 small pearl buttons

TENSION

20 sts and 30 rows = 10 cm (4 in.) square measured over lace pattern using 4 mm (US 6) knitting needles.

The ideal cover-up for those cool days in early spring, this feminine lacy cardigan is fastened with little pearl buttons.

BACK

Using 3 1/4 mm (US 3) needles, cast on 84 (88, 94, 98, 104, 108) sts and work 3 rows in garter st, ending with RS row.

Next row (WS): P2, *YO, P2tog, rep from * to end.

Work 4 rows in garter st, ending with WS row.

Change to 4 mm (US 6) needles and work in patt from chart on page 46, inc 1 st at each end of 5th row and every foll 12th row until there are 94 (98, 104, 108, 114, 118) sts, working inc sts in patt.

Work even until back measures 27 (28, 28, 29, 29, 30) cm [10 3/4 (11, 11, 11 1/2, 11 1/2, 11 3/4) in.], ending with WS row.

Shape armholes

Cast off 6 (6, 6, 6, 7, 7) sts in patt at beg next 2 rows: 82 (86, 92, 96, 100, 104) sts.

Dec 1 st at each end of next 3 (3, 5, 5, 5, 5) rows, then every other row 1 (2, 2, 3, 4, 5) times, then on every foll 4th row until 70 (72, 74, 76, 78, 80) sts rem.

Work even until armhole measures 20 (20, 21, 21, 22, 22) cm [8 (8, 8 1/4, 8 1/4, 8 3/4, 8 3/4) in.], ending with WS row.

Shape shoulders and back neck

Cast off 7 (7, 7, 7, 8, 8) sts at beg next 2 rows: 56 (58, 60, 62, 62, 64) sts.

Cast off 7 (7, 7, 7, 8, 8) sts, work in patt until there are 11 (11, 12, 12, 11, 12) sts on RH needle and turn, place rem sts on a holder.

Work both sides of neck separately.

Cast off 4 sts, purl to end.

Cast off rem 7 (7, 8, 8, 7, 8) sts.

With RS facing, rejoin yarn to sts from holder and cast off centre 20 (22, 22, 24, 24, 24) sts, work in patt to end.

Complete to match first side, reversing shaping and working an extra row before start of shoulder shaping.

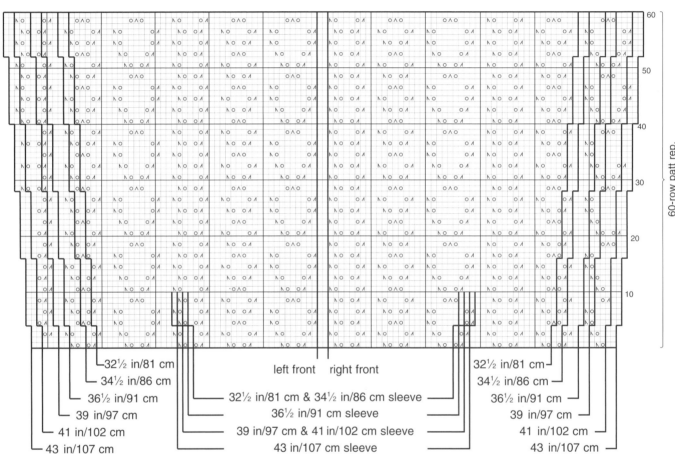

60

50

40

30

20

10

60-row patt rep.

32½ in/81 cm
34½ in/86 cm
36½ in/91 cm
39 in/97 cm
41 in/102 cm
43 in/107 cm

left front   right front

32½ in/81 cm & 34½ in/86 cm sleeve
36½ in/91 cm sleeve
39 in/97 cm & 41 in/102 cm sleeve
43 in/107 cm sleeve

32½ in/81 cm
34½ in/86 cm
36½ in/91 cm
39 in/97 cm
41 in/102 cm
43 in/107 cm

Key   ☐ K on RS, P on WS   ☉ YO   ☑ K2tog   ◹ K2tog tbl   ⅄ sl1, K2tog, psso

LEFT FRONT

Using 3¹/₄ mm (US 3) needles, cast on 43 (45, 47, 49, 53, 55) sts. Work 3 rows in garter st, end with RS row.

Next row (WS): P1, *YO, P2tog, rep from * to end.

Work 4 rows in garter st, inc 0 (0, 1, 1, 0, 0) sts at end of last row, and ending with WS row: 43 (45, 48, 50, 53, 55) sts.

Change to 4 mm (US 6) needles and cont in patt from chart, inc 1 st at beg of 5th row and every foll 12th row until there are 48 (50, 53, 55, 58, 60) sts, working inc sts in patt.

Work even until left front matches back to beg of armhole shaping, ending with WS row.

Shape armhole

Next row (RS): Keeping patt correct, cast off 6 (6, 6, 6, 7, 7) sts at beg of row: 42 (44, 47, 49, 51, 53) sts.

Work 1 row even.

Dec 1 st at armhole edge of next 3 (3, 5, 5, 5, 5) rows, then on every other row 1 (2, 2, 3, 4, 5) times, then on every foll 4th row until 36 (37, 38, 39, 40, 41) sts rem.

Work even until left front is 15 (15, 17, 17, 19, 19) rows shorter than back to start of shoulder shaping, ending with RS row.

Shape neck

Cast off 9 (10, 9, 10, 9, 9) sts at beg next row: 27 (27,29, 29, 31, 32) sts.

Dec 1 st at neck edge on next 4 rows, then on every other row 2 (2, 3, 3, 4, 4) times: 21 (21, 22, 22, 23, 24) sts.

Work 6 rows even, ending with WS row.

Shape shoulder

Cast off 7 (7, 7, 7, 8, 8) sts at beg next 2 RS rows.

Work 1 row even.

Cast off rem 7 (7, 8, 8, 7, 8) sts.

RIGHT FRONT

Using 3¹/₄ mm (US 3) needles, cast on 43 (45, 47, 49, 53, 55) sts and work 3 rows in garter st, ending with RS row.

Next row (WS): P1, *YO, P2tog, rep from * to end.

Work 4 rows in garter st, inc 0 (0, 1, 1, 0, 0) sts at beg of last

row, and ending with WS row: 43 (45, 48, 50, 53, 55) sts.

Change to 4 mm (US 6) needles and work in patt from chart, inc 1 st at end of 5th row and every foll 12th row until there are 48 (50, 53, 55, 58, 60) sts, working inc sts in patt.

Complete to match left front, reversing shaping and working an extra row before start of armhole, neck and shoulder shaping.

SLEEVES (work both the same)

Using 3¹/₄ mm (US 3) needles, cast on 47 (47, 49, 51, 51, 53) sts and work 3 rows in garter st, ending with RS row.

Next row (WS): P1, *YO, P2tog, rep from * to end.

Work 4 rows in garter st, inc 1 st at end of last row, and ending with WS row: 48 (48, 50, 52, 52, 54) sts.

Change to 4 mm (US 6) needles and cont in patt from chart, inc 1 st at each end of 5th row and every foll 14th (12th, 12th, 12th, 10th, 12th) row to 66 (64, 64, 66, 58, 76) sts, then on every foll 0 (14th, 14th, 14th, 12th, 0) row until there are 66 (68, 70, 72, 74, 76) sts, working inc sts in patt.

Work even until sleeve measures 46 (46, 47, 47, 47, 48) cm [18 (18, 18¹/₂, 18¹/₂, 18¹/₂, 19) in.], ending with WS row.

Shape sleevehead

Keeping patt correct, Cast off 6 (6, 6, 6, 7, 7) sts at beg of next 2 rows: 54 (56, 58, 60, 60, 62) sts.

Dec 1 st at each end of next 3 rows and then every other row twice: 44 (46, 48, 50, 50, 52) sts.

Work 3 rows even.

Dec 1 st at each end of next row and every foll 4th row until 34 (36, 38, 40, 38, 40) sts.

Work 1 row even.

Dec 1 st at each end of next row and then every other row 1 (2, 3, 4, 3, 4) times, then on every row until 20 sts rem.

Cast off 4 sts at beg next 2 rows.

Cast off rem 12 sts.

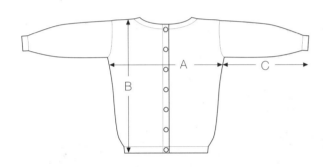

FINISHING

Press as described on page 21.

Join both shoulder seams.

Front bands (work both the same)

With RS facing and using 3¹/₄ mm (US 3) needles, pick up and knit 95 (97, 99, 101, 103, 105) sts along front opening edge between cast-on edge and neck shaping and work 2 rows in garter st, ending with RS row.

Next row (WS): P1, *YO, P2tog, rep from * to end.

Work 3 rows in garter st, ending with RS row.

Cast off knitwise on WS.

Neckband

With RS facing and using 3¹/₄ mm (US 3) needles, pick up and knit 27 (28, 29, 30, 31, 31) sts up right front neck, 27 (29, 29, 31, 31, 31) sts from back, 27 (28, 29, 30, 31, 31) sts down left front neck: 81 (85, 87, 91, 93, 93) sts.

Work 2 rows in garter st, ending with RS row.

Next row (WS): P1, *YO, P2tog, rep from * to end.

Work 3 rows in garter st, ending with RS row.

Cast off knitwise on WS.

Join side and sleeve seams.

Match centre of cast-off edge to shoulder seam.

Set in sleeve, easing sleevehead into armhole.

Sew buttons on to left front, spacing them evenly, and using eyelet holes of right front band as buttonholes.

fitted textured sweater

To fit bust size:					
81	86	91	97	102	107 cm
32	**34**	**36**	**38**	**40**	**42 in.**

Actual width at underarm (A):

86.5	92	97.5	102.5	108	112 cm
34	**36¼**	**38½**	**40½**	**42½**	**44 in.**

Finished length (B):

52	53	54	55	56	57 cm
20½	**21**	**21¼**	**21¾**	**22**	**22½ in.**

Sleeve length to underarm (C):

44	45	45	45	46	46 cm
17¼	**17¾**	**17¾**	**17¾**	**18**	**18 in.**

YARN

Variegated mohair version

50g balls of Impression (Kid mohair/polyamide),
#8 Brown Mix:

7	7	8	8	9	9

Solid angora version

50 g balls of Angora (Angora), #1 Buttermilk:

6	7	7	8	8	9

NEEDLES

Pair of 3¼ mm (US 3) knitting needles
Pair of 4 mm (US 6) knitting needles

TENSION

22 sts and 30 rows = 10 cm (4 in.) square measured over
st st using 4 mm (US 6) knitting needles.

Yarns can change the look of a garment. Here, the same sweater is knitted in a solid colour Angora and a variegated mohair-blend yarn.

BACK

Using 3¼ mm (US 3) needles, Cast off 95 (101, 107, 113, 119, 123) sts.

Work 2 rows in garter st, ending with WS row.

Begin RS, work in patt from chart on page 47 until chart row 20 has been completed, ending with WS row.

Change to 4mm (US 6) needles and, beg with a knit row, work 2 rows in st st.

Dec 1 st at each end of next row and every foll 6th row until there are 85 (91, 97, 103, 109, 113) sts.

Cont to work even until back measures 21 (22, 22, 23, 23, 24) cm [8¼ (8½, 8½, 9, 9, 9½) in.], ending with WS row.

Inc 1 st at each end of next row and every foll 6th row until there are 95 (101, 107, 113, 119, 123) sts.

Work even until back measures 34 (35, 35, 36, 36, 37) cm, [13¼ (13¾, 13¾, 14¼, 14¼, 14¾) in.] ending with WS row.

Shape armholes

Cast off 4 (5, 5, 6, 6, 6) sts at beg of next 2 rows, and 3 (3, 3, 4, 4, 4) sts at beg of foll 2 rows: 81 (85, 91, 93, 99, 103) sts.

Dec 1 st at each end of next 3 rows, and then on every other row until 73 (75, 77, 79, 83, 87) sts rem.

Work even until armhole measures 16 (16, 17, 17, 18, 18) cm [6½ (6½, 6¾, 6¾, 7, 7) in.], ending with WS row.

Shape back neck

Next row (RS): K26 (27, 28, 29, 31, 33) and turn, place rem sts on a holder.

Work each side of neck separately.

Next row: Cast off 6 sts, purl to end: 20 (21, 22, 23, 25, 27) sts.

Dec 1 st at neck edge on next 4 rows, ending with WS row.

Shape shoulder

Cast off 8 (8, 8, 9, 10, 11) sts at beg and dec 1 st at end of next row.

Work 1 row even.

Cast off rem 7 (8, 9, 9, 10, 11) sts.

With RS facing, rejoin yarn to rem sts and cast off centre 21 sts, knit to end.

Complete to match first side, reversing shaping and working an extra row before start of shoulder shaping.

FRONT

Work as for back until you have worked 20 rows fewer than on back to start of shoulder shaping, ending with WS row.

Shape front neck

Next row (RS): K28 (29, 30, 31, 33, 35) and turn, place rem sts on a holder.

Work each side of neck separately.

Next row: Cast off 4 sts, purl to end: 24 (25, 26, 27, 29, 31) sts.

Dec 1 st at neck edge on next 5 rows, then on every other row 4 times: 15 (16, 17, 18, 20, 22) sts.

Work 5 rows, ending with WS row.

Shape shoulder

Cast off 8 (8, 8, 9, 10, 11) sts at beg next row.

Work 1 row even.

Cast off rem 7 (8, 9, 9, 10, 11) sts.

With RS facing, rejoin yarn to rem sts and cast off centre 17 sts, knit to end.

Complete to match first side, reversing shaping and working an extra row before start of shoulder shaping.

SLEEVES (work both the same)

Using 3¼ mm (US 3) needles, cast on 57 (57, 59, 59, 61, 61) sts.

Work 2 rows in garter st, ending with WS row.

Work in patt from chart until chart row 20 has been completed, ending with WS row.

Change to 4 mm (US 6) needles and, beg with a knit row, work in st st as folls:

Inc 1 st at each end of next row and every foll 14th (14th, 14th, 14th, 12th, 12th) row to 73 (73, 65, 65, 71, 71) sts, then on

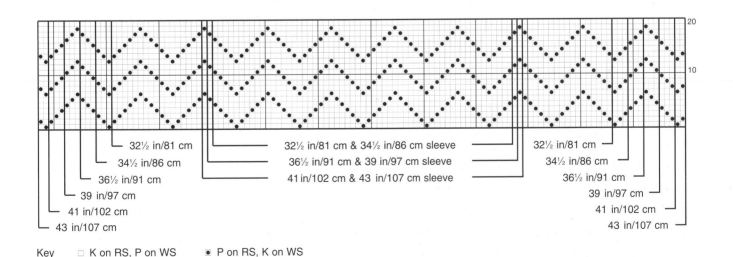

32½ in/81 cm

34½ in/86 cm

36½ in/91 cm

39 in/97 cm

41 in/102 cm

43 in/107 cm

32½ in/81 cm & 34½ in/86 cm sleeve

36½ in/91 cm & 39 in/97 cm sleeve

41 in/102 cm & 43 in/107 cm sleeve

32½ in/81 cm

34½ in/86 cm

36½ in/91 cm

39 in/97 cm

41 in/102 cm

43 in/107 cm

Key   □ K on RS, P on WS   ▣ P on RS, K on WS

every foll 0 (0, 12th, 12th, 10th, 10th) row until there are 73 (73, 77, 77, 81, 81) sts.

Work even until sleeve measures 44 (45, 45, 45, 46, 46) cm [17¹⁄₄ (17³⁄₄, 17³⁄₄, 17³⁄₄, 18, 18) in.], ending WS row.

Shape sleevehead

Cast off 5 sts at beg next 2 rows, and 3 sts at beg foll 2 rows: 57 (57, 61, 61, 65, 65) sts.

Dec 1 st at each end of next 3 then on every other row 3 times: 45 (45, 49, 49, 53, 53) sts.

Work 3 rows even.

Dec 1 st at each end of next row and on foll 4th row 3 times: 37 (37, 41, 41, 45, 45) sts.

Work 1 row even.

Dec 1 st at each end of next row and then on every other row twice, then on every foll row until 25 (25, 29, 29, 33, 33) sts rem.

Cast off 3 sts at beg of next 4 rows.

Cast off rem 13 (13, 17, 17, 21, 21) sts.

FINISHING

Press as described on page 21.

Join right shoulder seam.

Make neckband

With RS facing and using 3¹⁄₄ mm (US 3) needles, pick up and knit 23 sts down left front neck, 17 sts across centre front, 23 sts up right front neck, 12 sts down right back neck, 20 sts from back, and 12 sts up left back neck: 107 sts.

Next row (WS): P5, *K1, P11, rep from * to last 6 sts, K1, P5.

Next row: K4, *P1, K1, P1, K9, rep from * to last 7 sts, P1, K1, P1, K4.

Next row: P3, *K1, P3, K1, P7, rep from * to last 8 sts, K1, P3, K1, P3.

Next row: K2, * P1, K5, rep from * to last 3 sts, P1, K2.

Next row: P1, *K1, P7, K1, P3, rep from * to last 10 sts, K1, P7, K1, P1.

Next row: * P1, K9, P1, K1, rep from * ending last rep pl.

Next row: P11, *K1, P11, rep from * to end.

Knit 1 row.

Cast off knitwise on WS.

Join left shoulder and neckband seam.

Join side and sleeve seams.

Match centre of cast off edge to shoulder seam. Set in sleeve, easing sleevehead into armhole.

left: variegated mohair version

lace vest

This jumper is knitted in a lacy stitch with a moss stitch edging and looks great worn over another blouse or under a jacket.

To fit bust size:

81	86	91	97	102	107 cm
32	**34**	**36**	**38**	**40**	**42 in.**

Actual width at underarm (A):

87	91	97	101	107	111 cm
34¹/₄	**35³/₄**	**38¹/₄**	**39³/₄**	**42**	**43³/₄ in.**

Finished length (B):

45	45	47	47	49	49 cm
17³/₄	**17³/₄**	**18¹/₂**	**18¹/₂**	**19¹/₄**	**19¹/₄ in.**

YARN

25g balls of Kimono Angora (Angora/wool/nylon),
#1 Orange Mix:

4	4	4	5	5	5

NEEDLES

Pair of 3¹/₄ mm (US 3) knitting needles
Pair of 4 mm (US 6) knitting needles

GAUGE

20 sts and 30 rows = 10 cm (4 in.) square measured over lace pattern using 4 mm (US 6) knitting needles.

BACK

Using 3¹/₄ mm (US 3) needles, cast on 79 (83, 89, 93, 99, 103) sts.

Next row (RS): *K1, P1, rep from * to last st, K1.

Next row: *K1, P1, rep from * to last st, K1.

These 2 rows form moss st.

Work a further 2 rows in moss st, ending with WS row.

Change to 4 mm (US 6) needles and work in lace patt as folls:

Row 1 (RS): K4 (2, 1, 3, 2, 0), (YO, K2tog tbl, K2) 0 (1, 0, 0, 1, 0) times, *K1, K2tog, YO, K1, YO, K2tog tbl, K2, rep from * to last 3 (5, 0, 2, 5, 7) sts, (K1, K2tog, YO) 0 (1, 0, 0, 1, 1) times, K3 (2, 0, 2, 2, 1), (YO, K2tog tbl) 0 (0, 0, 0, 0, 1) times.

Rows 2 and 4: Purl.

Row 3: K1 (3, 1, 3, 3, 0), (YO, K2tog tbl, K1) 1 (1, 0, 0, 1, 0) times, *K2tog, YO, K3, YO, K2tog tbl, K1, rep from * to last 3 (5, 0, 2, 5, 7) sts, (K2tog, YO) 1 (1, 0, 0, 1, 1) times, K1 (3, 0, 2, 3, 3), (YO, K2tog tbl) 0 (0, 0, 0, 0, 1) times.

Row 5: K4 (1, 1, 3, 1, 0), (K2tog, YO, K3) 0 (1, 0, 0, 1, 0) times, *K2, YO, sl1, K2tog, psso, YO, K3, rep from * to last 3 (5, 0, 2, 5, 7) sts, K3 (2, 0, 2, 2, 2), (YO, K2tog tbl, K1) 0 (1, 0, 0, 1, 0) times, (YO, sl1, K2tog, psso, YO, K2) 0 (0, 0, 0, 0, 1) times.

Row 6: Purl.

These 6 rows form the lace pattern and are worked throughout.

Cont in lace patt, inc 1 st at each end of 7th row and every foll 12th row until there are 87 (91, 97, 101, 107, 111) sts, working inc sts in patt.

Work even until work measures 27 (27, 28, 28, 29, 29) cm [10³/₄ (10³/₄, 11, 11, 11¹/₂, 11¹/₂) in.], ending with WS row.

Shape armholes

Cast on 4 (5, 5, 6, 6, 7) sts at beg of next 2 rows, and 3 (3, 4, 4, 5, 5) sts at beg of foll 2 rows: 73 (75, 79, 81, 85, 87) sts.

Dec 1 st at each end of next row and then every other row until 67 (69, 71, 73, 75, 77) sts rem.

Work even until armhole measures 18 (18, 19, 19, 20, 20) cm [7 (7, 7½, 7½, 8, 8) in.], ending with WS row.

Shape shoulders and back neck

Cast off 4 (5, 5, 5, 6, 6) sts at beg of next row, work in patt until there are 9 (9, 10, 10, 10, 11) sts on RH needle and turn, place rem sts on a holder.

Work both sides of neck separately.

Cast off 4 sts, purl to end.

Cast off rem 5 (5, 6, 6, 6, 7) sts.

With RS facing, rejoin yarn to sts from holder, and cast off centre 41 (41, 41, 43, 43, 43) sts, work in patt to end.

Complete to match first side, reversing shaping.

FRONT

Work as given for back until you have worked 12 (12, 12, 14, 14, 14) rows fewer than on back to beg of shoulder shaping, ending with WS row.

Shape front neck

Next row (RS): Work in patt 21 (22, 23, 24, 25, 26) sts and turn, leaving rem sts on a holder.

Work each side of neck separately.

Cast off 4 sts at beg of next 2 WS rows.

Dec 1 st at neck edge on next 4 rows, then on every other row 0 (0, 0, 1, 1, 1) times: 9 (10, 11, 11, 12, 13) sts.

Work even until front matches back to start of shoulder shaping, ending with WS row.

Shape shoulder

Cast off 4 (5, 5, 5, 6, 6) sts at beg of next row.

Work 1 row even.

Cast off rem 5 (5, 6, 6, 6, 7) sts.

With RS facing, rejoin yarn to rem sts and cast off centre 25 sts, work in patt to end.

Complete to match first side, reversing shaping and working an extra row before start of shoulder shaping.

FINISHING

Press as described on page 21.

Join right shoulder seam.

Make neck edging

With RS facing and using 3¼ mm (US 3) needles, pick up and knit 17 (17, 17, 19, 19, 19) sts down left front neck, 25 sts across centre front, 17 (17, 17, 19, 19, 19) sts up right front neck, and 48 (48, 48, 50, 50, 50) sts across back neck: 107 (107, 107, 113, 113, 113) sts.

Work 2 rows in moss st.

Cast off in moss st on WS.

Join left shoulder and neck edging seam.

Armhole edgings (both alike)

With RS facing and using 3¼ mm (US 3) needles, pick up and knit 47 (47, 48, 48, 49, 49) sts to shoulder seam, then 48 (48, 49, 49, 50, 50) sts down to side seam: 95 (95, 97, 97, 99, 99) sts.

Work 2 rows in moss st as given for back.

Cast off in moss st on WS.

Join side and armhole edging seams.

twin set

An unusual contrast edging detail and deep rib bands add a modern twist to this classic cardigan and matching sleeveless shell.

Cardigan

BACK

Using 3¼ mm (3 US) needles and yarn CC, cast on 86 (90, 98, 102, 110, 114) sts.

Break off yarn CC and join yarn MC.

Rib row 1: [K2, P2] to last 2 sts, K2.

Rib row 2: [P2, K2] to last 2 sts, P2.

These 2 rows form rib.

Work in rib for a further 28 rows, dec 1 (0, 1, 0, 1, 1) st at each end of last row, ending with WS row. 84 (90, 96, 102, 108, 112) sts.

Change to 4 mm (US 6) needles.

Beg with a knit row, work st st for 2 (4, 4, 6, 6, 8) rows.

****Next row (RS) (inc):** K3, M1, knit to last 3 sts, M1, K3.

Working all incs set by last row, cont in st st, inc 1 st each end of every foll 12th row until there are 94 (100, 106, 112, 118, 122) sts.

Work even until back measures 31 (32, 32, 33, 33, 34) cm [12¼ (12½, 12½, 13, 13, 13½) in.], ending with WS row.

Shape armholes

Cast off 4 (5, 5, 6, 6, 6) sts at beg of next 2 rows, and 3 (3, 3, 4, 4, 4) sts at beg of foll 2 rows: 80 (84, 90, 92, 98, 102) sts.

Next row (RS) (dec): K3, K2tog, knit to last 5 sts, K2tog tbl, K3.

Next row (WS) (dec): P3, P2tog tbl, purl to last 5 sts, P2tog, P3.

Next row (RS) (dec): K3, K2tog, knit to last 5 sts, K2tog tbl, K3.

Working all decs as set by last row, dec 1 st at each end of every other row until 72 (74, 76, 78, 82, 86) sts rem.

Work even until armhole measures 19 (19, 20, 20, 21, 21) cm [7½ (7½, 8, 8, 8¼, 8¼) in.], ending with WS row.

To fit bust size:

81	86	91	97	102	107 cm
32	**34**	**36**	**38**	**40**	**42 in.**

CARDIGAN

Actual width at underarm (A):

85	91	96	102	107	111 cm
33½	**35¾**	**37¾**	**40**	**42**	**43¾ in.**

Finished length (B):

50	51	52	53	54	55 cm
19½	**20**	**20½**	**21**	**21¼**	**21¾ in.**

Sleeve length to underarm (C):

44	45	45	45	46	46 cm
17¼	**17¾**	**17¾**	**17¾**	**18**	**18 in.**

SHELL

Actual width at underarm (A):

87	91	97	101	107	111 cm
34¼	**35¾**	**38¼**	**39¾**	**42**	**43¾ in.**

Finished length (B):

49	50	51	52	53	54 cm
19¼	**19½**	**20**	**20½**	**21**	**21¼ in.**

YARN

Colour MC: 25g balls of Kimono Angora (Angora/wool/nylon), #8 Olive Mix:

Cardigan	8	8	9	9	10	10
Shell	4	5	5	6	6	7

Colour CC: 50g balls of Kimono Ribbon (Nylon), #8 Olive Mix:

Cardigan	1	1	1	1	1	1
Shell	1	1	1	1	1	1

NEEDLES

Pair of 3¼ mm (US 3) and 4 mm (US 6) knitting needles

BUTTONS

7 small pearl buttons

TENSION

22 sts and 30 rows = 10 cm (4 in.) square measured over st st using 4 mm (US 6) knitting needles.

Shape shoulders and back neck

Cast off 6 (6, 7, 7, 8, 8) sts beg next 2 rows: 60 (62, 62, 64, 66, 70) sts.

Cast off 6 (6, 7, 7, 8, 8) sts, knit until there are 9 (10, 9, 10, 10, 12) sts on RH needle and turn, place rem sts on a holder.

Work both sides of neck separately.

Cast off 3 sts, purl to end.

Cast off rem 6 (7, 6, 7, 7, 9) sts.

With RS facing, rejoin yarn to sts from holder, and cast off centre 30 sts, knit to end.

Complete to match first side, reversing shaping and working an extra row before start of shoulder shaping.

LEFT FRONT

Using 3¹/₄ mm (3 US) needles and yarn CC, cast on 46 (46, 50, 54, 58, 58) sts.

Break off yarn CC and join in yarn MC.

Rib row 1: (K2, P2) to last two sts, K2.

Rib row 2: (P2, K2) to last two sts, P2.

These 2 rows form rib.

Work in rib for a further 28 rows, dec 3 (0, 1, 2, 3, 1) sts evenly across last row, and ending with WS row: 43 (46, 49, 52, 55, 57) sts.

Change to 4 mm (US 6) needles.

Beg with a knit row, work in st st for 2 (4, 4, 6, 6, 8) rows.

Next row (RS) (inc): K3, M1, knit to end.

Working all incs as set by last row, cont in st st, inc 1 st at beg of every foll 12th row until there are 48 (51, 54, 57, 60, 62) sts.

Work even until left front matches back to beg of armhole shaping, end with WS row.

Shape armhole

Cast off 4 (5, 5, 6, 6, 6) sts at beg next row, and 3 (3, 3, 4, 4, 4) sts at beg foll RS row: 41 (43, 46, 47, 50, 52) sts.

Next row (RS) (dec): K3, K2tog, knit to end.

Next row (WS) (dec): Purl to last 5 sts, P2tog, P3.

Next row (RS) (dec): K3, K2tog, knit to end.

Working all decs as set by last row, dec 1 st at armhole edge of every other row until 37 (38, 39, 40, 42, 44) sts rem.

Work even until left front is 19 rows shorter than back to beg of shoulder shaping, end with RS row.

Shape neck

Cast off 12 sts at beg of next row: 25 (26, 27, 28, 30, 32) sts.

Dec 1 st at neck edge on next 3 rows, then every other row twice, then on every foll 4th row until 18 (19, 20, 21, 23, 25) sts rem.

Work 3 rows even, ending with WS row.

Shape shoulder

Cast off 6 (6, 7, 7, 8, 8) sts at beg of next 2 RS rows.

Work 1 row even.

Cast off rem 6 (7, 6, 7, 7, 9) sts.

RIGHT FRONT

Using 3¹/₄ mm (US 3) needles and yarn CC, cast on 46 (46, 50, 54, 58, 58) sts.

Break off yarn CC and join yarn MC..

Rib row 1: (K2, P2) to last 2 sts, K2.

Rib row 2: (P2, K2) to last 2 sts, P2.

These 2 rows form rib.

Work in rib for a further 28 rows, dec 3 (0, 1, 2, 3, 1) sts evenly across last row, and ending with RS facing for next row. 43 (46, 49, 52, 55, 57) sts.

Change to 4 mm (US 6) needles.

Beg with a knit row, work in st st for 2 (4, 4, 6, 6, 8) rows, ending with WS row.

Next row (RS) (inc): Knit to last 3 sts, M1, K3.

Working all incs as set by last row, cont in st st, inc 1 st at end of every foll 12th row until there are 48 (51, 54, 57, 60, 62) sts. Complete to match left front, reversing shaping and working an extra row before start of armhole, neck and shoulder shaping.

SLEEVES (work both the same)

Using 3¼ mm (US 3) needles and yarn CC, cast on 56 (56, 58, 58, 60, 60) sts.

Break off yarn CC and join yarn MC.

Rib row 1: P1 (1, 0, 0, 1, 1), (K2, P2) 13 (13, 14, 14, 14, 14) times, K2, P1 (1, 0, 0, 1, 1).

Rib row 2: K1 (1, 0, 0, 1, 1), (P2, K2) 13 (13, 14, 14, 14, 14) times, P2, K1 (1, 0, 0, 1, 1).

These 2 rows form rib.

Work in rib for further 28 rows, inc 1 st each end of 13th and foll 14th rows, ending with WS row: 60 (60, 62, 62, 64, 64) sts. Change to 4 mm (US 6) needles.

Beg with a knit row, work in st st for 12 (12, 12, 12, 10, 10) rows.

Next row (RS) (inc): K3, M1, knit to last 3 sts, M1, K3.

Working all incs as set by last row, cont in st st, inc 1 st at each end of every foll 14th (14th, 12th, 12th, 12th, 12th) to 72 (72, 76, 76, 70, 70) sts, then on every foll 0 (0, 0, 0, 10th, 10th) row until there are 72 (72, 76, 76, 80, 80) sts.

Work even until sleeve measures 44 (45, 45, 45, 46, 46) cm [17¼ (17¾, 17¾, 17¾, 18, 18) in.], end with WS row.

Shape sleevehead

Cast off 5 sts at beg of next 2 rows, and 3 sts at beg foll 2 rows: 56 (56, 60, 60, 64, 64) sts.

Dec 1 st at each end of next 3 rows and then every other row 3 times: 44 (44, 48, 48, 52, 52) sts.

Work 3 rows even, then dec 1 st at each end of next row and foll 4th row 3 times: 36 (36, 40, 40, 44, 44) sts.

Work 1 row even, then dec 1 st at each end of next row and then every other row twice, then on every row until 24 (24, 28, 28, 32, 32) sts rem.

Cast off 3 sts at beg of next 4 rows.

Cast off rem 12 (12, 16, 16, 20, 20) sts.

FINISHING

Press as described on page 21.

Join both shoulder seams.

Make neckband

With RS facing and using 3¼ mm (US 3) needles and yarn MC, pick up and knit 31 sts up right front neck, 36 sts from back, and then 31 sts down left front neck: 98 sts.

Rib row 1: [K2, P2] to last 2 sts, K2.

Rib row 2: [P2, K2] to last 2 sts, P2.

Rep these 2 rows once more.

Cast off in rib on WS.

Make buttonhole band

With RS facing and using 3¼ mm (US 3) needles and yarn MC, pick up and knit 102 (102, 106, 106, 110, 110) sts along right front opening edge.

Next row (WS): (P2, K2) to last 2 sts, P2.

Next row (buttonhole row): Rib 3, YO, work 2tog, [rib 16 (16, 17, 17, 18, 18), YO, work 2tog] 3 times, rib 15 (15, 16, 16, 17, 17), [YO, work 2tog, rib 10] twice, YO, work 2tog, rib 2.

Work a further 2 rows in rib.

Cast off in rib on WS.

Make button band

With RS facing and using 3¼ mm (US 3) needles and yarn MC, pick up and knit 102 (102, 106, 106, 110, 110) sts along left front opening edge.

Next row (WS): [P2, K2] to last 2 sts, P2.

Next row: [K2, P2] to last 2 sts, K2.

Rep these 2 rows once more.

Cast off in rib on WS.

Join side and sleeve seams.

Match centre of cast off edge to shoulder seam. Set in sleeve, easing sleevehead into armhole. Sew on buttons.

Shell

BACK

Using 3¹⁄₄ mm (US 3) needles and yarn CC, cast on 86 (90, 98, 102, 110, 114) sts.

Break off yarn CC and join yarn MC.

Rib row 1: [K2, P2] to last 2 sts, K2.

Rib row 2: [P2, K2] to last 2 sts, P2.

These 2 rows form rib.

Work in rib for a further 28 rows, dec 1 (0, 1, 0, 1, 1) sts at each end of last row, and ending with WS row: 84 (90, 96, 102, 108, 112) sts.

Change to 4 mm (US 6) needles.

Beg with a knit row, cont in st st for 2 rows.

**Next row (RS) (inc): K3, M1, knit to last 3 sts, M1, K3.

Working all incs set by last row, cont in st st, inc 1 st each end of every foll 12th row until there are 94 (100, 106, 112, 118, 122) sts.

Work even until back measures 31 (32, 32, 33, 33, 34) cm [12¹⁄₄ (12¹⁄₂, 12¹⁄₂, 13, 13, 13¹⁄₂) in.], ending with WS row.

Shape armholes

Cast off 4 (5, 5, 6, 6, 6) sts at beg next 2 rows, and 3 (3, 3, 4, 4, 4) sts at beg foll 2 rows: 80 (84, 90, 92, 98, 102) sts.

Next row (RS) (dec): K3, K2tog, knit to last 5 sts, K2tog tbl, K3.

Next row (WS) (dec): P3, P2tog tbl, purl to last 5 sts, P2tog, P3.

Next row (RS) (dec): K3, K2tog, knit to last 5 sts, K2tog tbl, K3.

Working all decs as set by last row, dec 1 st at each end of every other row until 72 (74, 76, 78, 82, 86) sts rem.

Cont without shaping till armhole measures 19 (19, 20, 20, 21, 21) cm [7¹⁄₂ (7¹⁄₂, 8, 8, 8¹⁄₄, 8¹⁄₄) in.], ending with WS row.

Shape shoulders and back neck

Cast off 6 (6, 7, 7, 8, 8) sts at beg of next 2 rows: 60 (62, 62, 64, 66, 70) sts.

Cast off 6 (6, 7, 7, 8, 8) sts, knit until there are 9 (10, 9, 10, 10, 12) sts on RH needle and turn, place rem sts on a holder.

Work both sides of neck separately.

Cast off 3 sts, purl to end.

Cast off rem 6 (7, 6, 7, 7, 9) sts.

With RS facing, rejoin yarn to sts from holder and cast off centre 30 sts, knit to end.

Complete to match first side, reversing shaping and working an extra row before start of shoulder shaping.

FRONT

Work as for back until you have worked 18 rows fewer than on back to beg of shoulder shaping, ending with WS row.

Shape front neck

Next row (RS): K28 (29, 30, 31, 33, 35) and turn, place rem sts on a holder.

Next row: Cast off 4 sts, purl to end: 24 (25, 26, 27, 29, 31) sts. Dec 1 st at neck edge on next 3 rows, then on foll alt row, then on every foll 4th row until 18 (19, 20, 21, 23, 25) sts rem. Work 3 rows even, ending with RS facing for next row.

Shape shoulder

Cast off 6 (6, 7, 7, 8, 8) sts at beg of next 2 RS rows.

Work 1 row even.

Cast off rem 6 (7, 6, 7, 7, 9) sts.

With RS facing, rejoin yarn to rem sts and cast off centre 16 sts, knit to end.

Complete to match first side, reversing shaping and working an extra row before start of shoulder shaping.

FINISHING

Press as described on page 21.

Join right shoulder seam.

Make neck edging

With RS facing and using 3 1/4 mm (US 3) needles and yarn MC, pick up and knit 22 sts down left front neck, 16 sts across centre front, 22 sts up right front neck, and 36 sts across back neck: 96 sts.

Next row: [K2, P2] to end.

Rep last row 3 times more.

Cast off in rib on WS.

Join left shoulder and neck edging seam.

Make armhole edgings (both alike)

With RS facing and using 3 1/4 mm (US 3) needles and yarn MC, pick up and knit 51 (51, 55, 55, 57, 57) sts to shoulder seam, then 51 (51, 55, 55, 57, 57) sts down to side seam: 102 (102, 110, 110, 114, 114) sts.

Rib row 1: K2, [P2, K2] to end.

Rib row 2: P2, [K2, P2] to end.

Rep last 2 rows once more.

Cast off in rib on WS. Join side and armhole edging seams.

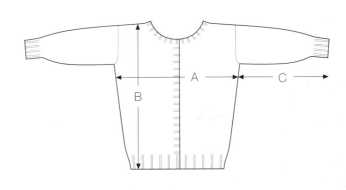

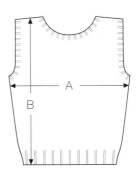

cotton

nautical stripe sweater

To fit bust size:

32	34	36	38	40	42 in.
81	86	91	97	102	107 cm

Actual width at underarm (A):

35³/₄	38¹/₄	39³/₄	42	43³/₄	46 in.
91	97	101	107	111	117 cm

Finished length (B):

19³/₄	20	20¹/₂	21	21¹/₄	21³/₄ in.
50	51	52	53	54	55 cm

Sleeve length to underarm (C):

17¹/₄	17³/₄	17³/₄	17³/₄	18	18 in.
44	45	45	45	46	46 cm

YARN

50 g balls of Nautical Cotton (Cotton)

Color MC: Natural

9	9	10	10	11	12

Color CC1: Navy

2	2	3	3	3	4

Color CC2: Red

1	1	1	1	1	1

NEEDLES

Pair of US 5 (3³/₄ mm) knitting needles

Pair of US 7 (4¹/₂ mm) knitting needles

TENSION

20 sts and 28 rows = 10 cm (4 in.) square measured over St st using 4¹/₂ mm (US 7) knitting needles.

Blue-and-white is always a fresh color combination, but this jaunty nautical-style sweater also has a bright red edging for extra zing.

BACK

Using US 5 (3³/₄ mm) needles and yarn CC2, cast on 83 (89, 93, 99, 101, 109) sts. Knit 6 rows, ending with WS row. Break off yarn CC2.

Change to 4¹/₂ mm (US 7) needles.

Beg with a knit row, work in striped St st as folls:

Join yarns MC and CC1 and work 12 rows in MC, and then 2 rows in CC1.

These 14 rows form the main stripe patt and are repeated.

Cont in stripe patt, inc 1 st at each end of next row and every foll 14th (14th, 14th, 16th, 16th, 16th) row until there are 91 (97, 101, 107, 111, 117) sts.

Work even in stripe patt until work measures 30 (31, 31, 32, 32, 33) cm [11³/₄ (12¹/₄, 12¹/₄, 12¹/₂, 12¹/₂, 13) in.], ending with WS row.

Shape armholes

Cast off 6 (6, 7, 7, 8, 8) sts at beg next 2 rows: 79 (85, 87, 93, 95, 101) sts.

Work in medium stripe patt (6 rows MC, then 2 rows CC1), dec 1 st at each end of next 3 (5, 5, 7, 7, 9) rows, then on every other row twice, and then on every foll 4th row until 67 (69, 71, 73, 75, 77) sts rem.

Work even in medium stripe patt until armhole measures 12 (12, 13, 13, 14, 14) cm [4³/₄ (4³/₄, 5, 5, 5¹/₂, 5¹/₂) in.], ending with WS row.

Now work in stripe patt (2 rows MC, then 2 rows CC1), until armhole measures 20 (20, 21, 21, 22, 22) cm [8 (8, 8¹/₄, 8¹/₄, 8³/₄, 8³/₄) in.], ending with WS row.

Shape shoulders and back neck

Keeping patt correct, cast off 4 (4, 5, 5, 5, 6) sts at beg of next row, knit until there are 9 (10, 10, 10, 11, 11) sts on RH needle, then turn and place rem sts on a holder.

Work both sides of neck separately.

Cast off 5 sts, purl to end. Cast off rem 4 (5, 5, 5, 6, 6) sts.

With RS facing, rejoin yarn to sts from holder and cast off centre 41 (41, 41, 43, 43, 43) sts, knit to end.

Complete to match first side, reversing shaping and working an extra row before beg of shoulder shaping.

FRONT

Work as for back until you have worked 8 (8, 8, 10, 10, 10) rows fewer on back to beg of shoulder shaping, ending with WS row.

Shape neck

Next row (RS): K21 (22, 23, 24, 25, 26) and turn, place rem sts on a holder.

Next row: Cast off 9 sts, purl to end.

Dec 1 st at neck edge on next 3 rows, then on every other row 1 (1, 1, 2, 2, 2) times: 8 (9, 10, 10, 11, 12) sts.

Work even until front matches back to beg of shoulder shaping, ending with WS row.

Shape shoulder

Cast off 4 (4, 5, 5, 5, 6) sts at beg of row.

Work 1 row even and cast off rem 4 (5, 5, 5, 6, 6) sts.

With RS facing, rejoin yarn to sts from holder and cast off centre 25 sts, knit to end.

Complete to match first side, reversing shaping.

SLEEVES (work both the same)

Using 3³/₄ mm (US 5) needles and yarn CC2, cast on 49 (49, 51, 51, 51, 53) sts and knit 6 rows, ending with WS row. Break off yarn CC2.

Change to 4¹/₂ mm (US 7) needles.

Join in yarns MC and CC1.

Beg with a knit row, work in sleeve stripe patt (10 rows MC, followed by 2 rows CC1), at the same time inc 1 st at each end of the 3rd and every foll 14th (12th, 12th, 10th, 10th, 10th) row to 55 (61, 63, 73, 65, 67) sts, then on every foll 12th (10th,

10th, 0, 8th, 8th) row until there are 67 (69, 71, 73, 75, 77) sts.

Work without further shaping until sleeve measures 44 (45, 45, 45, 46, 46) cm [17¹/₄ (17³/₄, 17³/₄, 17³/₄, 18, 18) in], end with WS row.

Shape sleevehead

Cast off 6 (6, 7, 7, 8, 8) sts at beg next 2 rows: 55 (57, 57, 59, 59, 61) sts.

Dec 1 st at each end of next 5 rows, then on foll alt row, then on every foll 4th row until 33 (35, 35, 37, 37, 39) sts rem.

Work 1 row even.

Dec 1 st at each end of next row and every other row 1 (1, 2, 2, 3, 3) times, then on foll 3 rows.

Cast off 5 sts at beg of next 2 rows.

Cast off rem 13 (15, 13, 15, 13, 15) sts.

FINISHING

Press as described on page 21.

Join right shoulder seam.

Make neck edging

With RS facing and 3³/₄ mm (US 5) needles and yarn CC2, pick up 17 (17, 17, 18, 18, 18) sts down left neck, 25 sts from front, 17 (17, 17, 18, 18, 18) sts up right neck, 51 (51, 51, 53, 53, 53) sts from back: 110 (110, 110, 114, 114, 114) sts.

Knit 2 rows.

Bind off.

Join left shoulder and neckband.

Join side and sleeve seams.

Match centre of cast off edge to shoulder, set in sleeve.

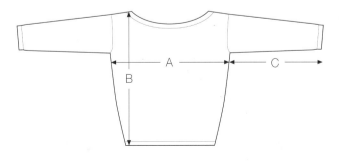

shawl-collar jacket

To fit bust size:					
81	86	91	97	102	107 cm
32	**34**	**36**	**38**	**40**	**42 in.**

Actual width at underarm (A):

91	97	101	107	111	117 cm
36	**38**	**39³/₄**	**42**	**44**	**46 in.**

Finished length (B):

49	50	51	52	53	54 cm
19¹/₄	**19³/₄**	**20**	**20¹/₂**	**21**	**21¹/₄ in.**

Sleeve length to underarm (C):

44	45	45	45	46	46 cm
17¹/₄	**17³/₄**	**17³/₄**	**17³/₄**	**18**	**18 in.**

YARN

50 g balls of Fauve (Nylon)

Colour MC: Chocolate

12	12	13	13	14	14

Colour CC: Beige

3	3	3	4	4	4

NEEDLES

Pair of 5¹/₂ mm (US 9) knitting needles
Pair of 6¹/₂ mm (US 10¹/₂) knitting needles

BUTTONS

5 medium buttons to match yarn CC

TENSION

20 sts and 28 rows = 10 cm (4 in. square measured over st st using 6¹/₂ mm (US 10¹/₂) knitting needles.

This garment is knit in a modern nylon ribbon yarn, that has the same tension as a cotton DK. Simply adjust the needle size as suggested on ball band.

BACK

Using 5¹/₂ mm (US 9) needles and yarn MC, cast on 83 (89, 93, 99, 103, 109) sts. Knit 4 rows, ending with WS row.

Change to 6¹/₂ mm (US 10¹/₂) needles.

Beg with a knit row, work in st st for 14 rows.

Next row (RS) (inc): K3, M1, knit to last 3 sts, M1, K3.

Working all incs as set by last row, cont in st st, inc 1 st at each end of every foll 14th row until there are 91 (97, 101, 107, 111, 117) sts.

Work even until back measures 30 (31, 31, 32, 32, 33) cm [11³/₄ (12¹/₄, 12¹/₄, 12¹/₂, 12¹/₂, 13) in.], ending with WS row.

Shape armholes

Cast off 4 (5, 5, 6, 6, 7) sts at beg of next 2 rows, and cast off 3 sts at beg foll 2 rows: 77 (81, 85, 89, 93, 97) sts.

Next row (RS) (dec): K3, K2tog tbl, knit to last 5 sts, K2tog, K3.

Working all decs as set by last row, dec 1 st at each end of every other row until 67 (71, 73, 77, 81, 83) sts rem.

Work even until armhole measures 19 (19, 20, 20, 21, 21) cm [7¹/₂ (7¹/₂, 8, 8, 8¹/₄, 8¹/₄) in.], ending with WS row.

Shape shoulders and back neck

Cast off 6 (7, 7, 8, 8, 9) sts at beg of next 2 rows: 55 (57, 59, 61, 65, 65) sts.

Next row (RS): Cast off 6 (7, 7, 8, 8, 9) sts, knit until there are 9 (9, 10, 10, 12, 11) sts on right needle and turn, place rem sts on a holder.

Work both sides of neck separately.

Cast off 3 sts, purl to end. Cast off rem 6 (6, 7, 7, 9, 8) sts.

With RS facing rejoin yarn to sts from holder, cast off centre 25 sts, knit to end.

Complete to match first side, reversing shaping and working an extra row before beg of shoulder shaping.

LEFT FRONT

Using 5¹⁄₂ mm (US 9) needles and yarn MC, cast on 42 (45, 47, 50, 52, 55) sts. Knit 4 rows, ending with WS row.

Change to 6¹⁄₂ mm (US 10¹⁄₂) needles.

Beg with a knit row, work in st st for 14 rows.

Next row (RS) (inc): K3, M1, knit to end.

Working all incs as set by last row, cont in st st, inc 1 st at beg of every foll 14th row until there are 46 (49, 51, 54, 56, 59) sts. Work even until left front matches back to beg of armhole shaping, ending with WS row.

Shape armhole and front neck

Cast off 4 (5, 5, 6, 6, 7) sts at beg and dec 1 st at end of next row.

Work 1 row even.

Bind off 3 sts at beg and dec 1 st at end of next row: 37 (39, 41, 43, 45, 47) sts.

Work 1 row even.

Next row (RS) (dec): K3, K2tog tbl, knit to last 5 sts, K2tog, K3.

Working all decs as set by last row, dec 1 st at each end of every other row until 27 (29, 29, 31, 31, 33) sts rem.

Work 1 (1, 1, 1, 1, 3) rows, ending with WS row.

Dec 1 st at neck edge only of next row and every foll 4th row until 18 (20, 21, 23, 25, 26) sts rem.

Work even until left front matches back to start of shoulder shaping, ending with WS row.

Shape shoulder

Cast off 6 (7, 7, 8, 8, 9) sts at beg of next 2 RS rows.

Work 1 row even.

Cast off rem 6 (6, 7, 7, 9, 8) sts.

RIGHT FRONT

Using 5¹⁄₂ mm (US 9) needles and yarn MC, cast on 42 (45, 47, 50, 52, 55) sts. Knit 4 rows, ending with WS row.

Change to 6¹⁄₂ mm (US 10¹⁄₂) needles.

Beg with a knit row, work in st st for 14 rows.

Next row (RS) (inc): Knit to last 3 sts, M1, K3.

Working all incs as set by last row, cont in st st, inc 1 st at end of every foll 14th row until there are 46 (49, 51, 54, 56, 59) sts. Complete to match left front, reversing shaping and working an extra row before beg armhole and shoulder shaping.

SLEEVES (work both the same)

Using 5¹⁄₂ mm (US 9) needles and yarn MC, cast on 51 (51, 53, 53, 55, 55) sts. Knit 2 rows, ending with WS row.

Change to 6¹⁄₂ mm (US 10¹⁄₂) needles.

Beg with a knit row, work 16 (16, 14, 14, 12, 12) rows in st st, ending with WS row.

Next row (RS) (inc): K3, M1, knit to last 3 sts, M1, K3.

Working all incs as set by last row, cont in st st, inc 1 st at each end of every foll 18th (18th, 16th, 16th, 14th, 14th) row to 55 (55, 57, 57, 65, 64) sts, then on every foll 16th (16th, 14th, 14th, 12th, 12th) row until there are 63 (63, 67, 67, 71, 71) sts. Work even until sleeve measures 44 (45, 45, 45, 46, 46) cm [17¹⁄₄ (17³⁄₄, 17³⁄₄, 17³⁄₄, 18, 18) in.], ending with WS row.

Shape sleevehead

Cast off 5 sts at beg next 2 rows, and 3 sts at beg foll 2 rows: 47 (47, 51, 51, 55, 55) sts.

Dec 1 st at each end of next 3 rows, work 1 row even, and then work 1 more row with dec: 39 (39, 43, 43, 47, 47) sts.

Work 3 rows even.

Dec1 st at each end of next row and foll 4th row 5 times: 27 (27, 31, 31, 35, 35) sts.

Work 1 row even.

Dec 1 st at each end of next 2 rows: 23 (23, 27, 27, 31, 31) sts.

Cast off 3 sts at beg next 4 rows: 11 (11, 15, 15, 19, 19) sts.

Cast off rem sts.

FINISHING

Press as described on page 21.

Join shoulder seams.

Make buttonhole band

With RS facing and starting at cast-on edge of right front, using 5¹/₂ mm (US 9) needles and yarn MC, pick up 61 (61, 61, 65, 65, 65) sts to start of neck shaping.

Knit 1 row, ending with WS row.

Next row (RS) (buttonhole row): K2, *K2tog, YO, K12 (12, 12, 13, 13, 13), rep from * to last 3 sts, K2tog, YO, K1.

Knit 2 rows.

Cast off knitwise on WS.

Make button band

Work as for buttonhole band, picking up sts along left front opening edge and omitting buttonholes.

Make cuffs (work both the same)

Using 5¹/₂ mm (US 9) needles and yarn CC, cast on 53 (53, 55, 55, 57, 57) sts.

Next row 1 (RS): *K1, P1, rep from * to last st, K1.

Rep this row until cuff measures 10 cm (4 in.), ending with RS row.

Cast off knitwise on WS.

Make left front collar

With RS facing and using 5¹/₂ mm (US 9) needles and yarn CC, pick up and knit 3 sts across top of button band and work in moss st as for cuffs as folls:

Work 2 rows, ending with RS of collar (when being worn) facing for next row.

Inc 1 st at beg of next row and every other row 11 times, then every foll 4th row until there are 24 sts, working inc sts in moss st.

Cont in moss st until collar fits up left front neck and around to centre back, ending with WS of collar facing for next row.

Shape back of collar

Cast off 8 sts at beg of next 2 RS rows.

Work 1 row even.

Cast off rem 8 sts.

Make right front collar

Work as given for left front collar, picking up sts across top of buttonhole band and reversing shaping.

Stitch collar sections neatly in place.

Join collar at centre back neck.

Join side and sleeve seams.

Match centre of cast off edge of sleeve to shoulder seam. Set in sleeve, easing sleevehead into armhole.

Join row-end edges of cuffs to form a loop. With RS facing, stitch cuffs neatly in place around lower edge of sleeves, matching seams.

Sew on buttons to correspond with buttonholes.

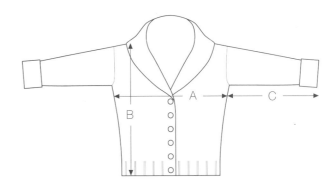

fair isle sweater

To fit bust size:					
81	86	91	97	102	107 cm
32	**34**	**36**	**38**	**40**	**42 in.**
Actual width at underarm (A):					
99	103	109	113	119	123 cm
39	**40$^1/_2$**	**43**	**44$^1/_2$**	**46$^3/_4$**	**48$^1/_2$ in.**
Finished length (B):					
48	48	51	51	54	54 cm
19	**19**	**20**	**20**	**21$^1/_4$**	**21$^1/_4$ in.**
Sleeve length to underarm (C):					
46	46	47	47	48	48 cm
18	**18**	**18$^1/_2$**	**18$^1/_2$**	**19**	**19 in.**

YARN

50g balls of Nautical Cotton (Cotton)

Colour MC: Black					
10	10	11	11	12	13
Colour CC1: Beige					
2	2	2	2	2	2
Colour CC2: Lime					
2	2	2	2	3	3
Colour CC3: Ecru					
2	2	2	2	2	2

NEEDLES

Pair of 3$^3/_4$ mm (US 5) knitting needles

Pair of 4$^1/_2$ mm (US 7) knitting needles

TENSION

20 sts and 28 rows = 10 cm (4 in.) square measured over st st using 4$^1/_2$ mm (US 7) knitting needles.

This loose-fitting top with a plain V-neck features a distinctive wide band of intricate Fair Isle stitching across the bottom of the body and the sleeves.

BACK

Using 3$^3/_4$ mm (US 5) needles and yarn MC, cast on 99 (103, 109, 113, 119, 123) sts. Work 10 rows in garter st, ending with WS row.

Change to 4$^1/_2$ mm (US 7) needles.

Joining in and breaking off contrast shades as required, work 37 rows in patt from chart on page 78, which is worked in st st using the Fair Isle technique (see page 18), ending with RS row.

Next row (WS): Beg with a purl row, work in st st in yarn MC until back measures 29 (29, 31, 31, 33, 33) cm [11$^1/_2$ (11$^1/_2$, 12$^1/_4$, 12$^1/_4$, 13, 13) in.], ending with WS row.

Shape armholes

Cast off 5 (6, 6, 7, 7, 8) sts at beg next 2 rows, then 4 (4, 5, 5, 6, 6) sts at beg foll 2 rows: 81 (83, 87, 89, 93, 95) sts.**

Dec 1 st at each end of next row and then every other row 4 (4, 5, 5, 6, 6) times: 71 (73, 75, 77, 79, 81) sts.

Work even until armhole measures 19 (19, 20, 20, 21, 21) cm [7$^1/_2$ (7$^1/_2$, 8, 8, 8$^1/_4$, 8$^1/_4$) in.], ending with WS row.

Shape shoulders and back neck

Cast off 7 (7, 7, 7, 8, 8) sts at beg of next 2 rows: 57 (59, 61, 63, 63, 65) sts.

Next row (RS): Cast off 7 (7, 7, 7, 8, 8) sts at beg of next row, knit until there are 10 (11, 12, 12, 11, 12) sts on RH needle and turn, place rem sts on a holder.

Work both sides of neck separately.

Cast off 4 sts, purl to end.

Cast off rem 6 (7, 8, 8, 7, 8) sts.

With RS facing, rejoin yarn to sts from holder and cast off centre 23 (23, 23, 25, 25, 25) sts, knit to end.

Complete to match first side, reversing shaping.

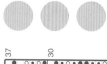

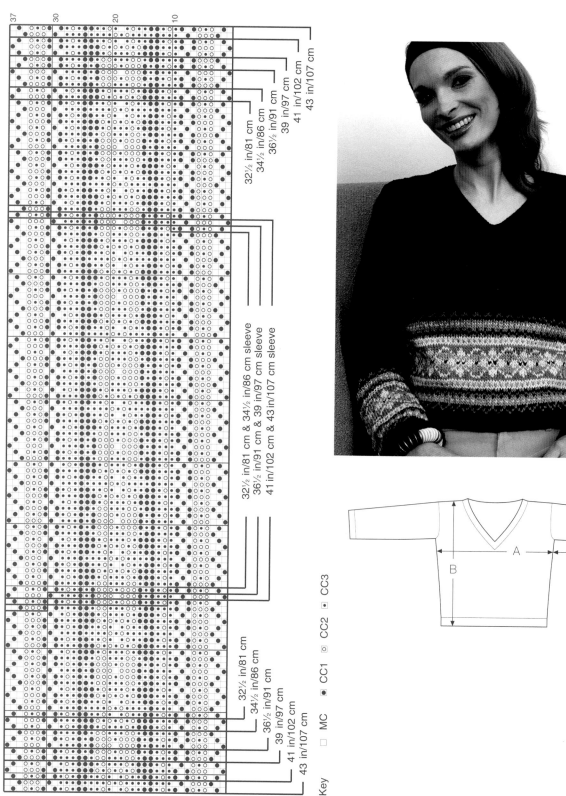

37   30   20   10

32½ in/81 cm
34½ in/86 cm
36½ in/91 cm
39 in/97 cm
41 in/102 cm
43 in/107 cm

32½ in/81 cm & 34½ in/86 cm sleeve
36½ in/91 cm & 39 in/97 cm sleeve
41 in/102 cm & 43in/107 cm sleeve

32½ in/81 cm
34½ in/86 cm
36½ in/91 cm
39 in/97 cm
41 in/102 cm
43 in/107 cm

Key   □ MC   ◉ CC1   ◎ CC2   ⊡ CC3

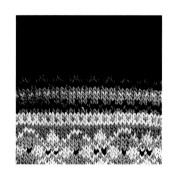

FRONT

Work as given for back to **, ending with WS row.

Dec 1 st at each end of next row and then every other row 3 (3, 4, 4, 5, 5) times: 73 (75, 77, 79, 81, 83) sts.

Shape neck

Next row (RS): K2tog, knit until there are 34 (35, 36, 37, 38, 39) sts on RH needle, K2tog tbl and turn, place rem sts on a holder: 35 (36, 37, 38, 39, 40) sts.

Work 1 row even.

Dec at end of next row and then every other row 13 (13, 13, 14, 14, 14) times, and then on every foll 4th row until 20 (21, 22, 22, 23, 24) sts rem.

Work even until front matches back to beg of shoulder shaping, ending with WS row.

Shape shoulder

Cast off 7 (7, 7, 7, 8, 8) sts at beg of next 2 RS rows.

Work 1 row even.

Cast off rem 6 (7, 8, 8, 7, 8) sts.

With RS facing, rejoin yarn to sts from holder, knit to last 2 sts, K2tog tbl: 35 (36, 37, 38, 39, 40) sts.

Complete to match first side, reversing shaping and working an extra row before start of shoulder shaping.

SLEEVES (work both the same)

Using 3 3/4 mm (US 5) needles and yarn MC, cast on 57 (57, 59, 59, 61, 61) sts and work 10 rows in garter st, ending with WS row.

Change to 4 1/2 mm (US 7) needles and work in Fair Isle patt from chart, inc 1 st at each end of 11th row and foll 20th row, and ending with RS row.

Next row (WS): Beg with a purl row, work in st st, inc 1 st at each end of every foll 20th row from previous inc until there are 67 (67, 69, 69, 71, 71) sts.

Work even until sleeve measures 46 (46, 47, 47, 48, 48) cm [18 (18, 18 1/2, 18 1/2, 19, 19) in.], ending with WS row.

Shape sleevehead

Cast off 5 sts at beg next 2 rows: 57 (57, 59, 59, 61, 61) sts.

Dec 1 st at each end of next 3 rows, then on every other row 3 times, and then on every foll 4th row until 37 (37, 39, 39, 41, 41) sts rem.

Work 1 row even.

Dec 1 st at each end of next row and then on every other row 2 (2, 3, 3, 4, 4) times, then on 3 foll rows.

Cast off 3 sts at beg of next 4 rows.

Cast off rem 13 sts.

FINISHING

Press as described on page 21.

Join right shoulder seam.

Make neckband

With RS facing and using 3 3/4 mm (US 5) needles and yarn MC, pick up and knit 37 (37, 39, 39, 40, 40) sts down left front neck, 1 st from centre and mark this st, 37 (37, 39, 39, 40, 40) sts up right front neck, and 31 (31, 31, 33, 33, 33) sts across back neck: 106 (106, 110, 112, 114, 114) sts.

Next row (WS): Knit to within 2 sts of marked st, K2tog, K1, K2tog tbl, knit to end.

Next row: Knit.

Cast off knitwise on WS, dec 2 sts at center front as before.

Join left shoulder and neckband seam.

Join side and sleeve seams.

Match centre of cast off edge to shoulder seam.

Set in sleeve, easing sleevehead into armhole.

fitted cardigan

The elegant look of this stylish cardigan depends on it being a perfect fit, so check all the measurements and your tension carefully before you begin.

To fit bust size:					
81	86	91	97	102	107 cm
32	**34**	**36**	**38**	**40**	**42 in.**

Actual width at underarm (A):					
87	91	97	101	107	111 cm
34¼	**35¾**	**38¼**	**39¾**	**42**	**43¾ in.**

Finished length (B):					
52	53	54	55	56	57 cm
20½	**21**	**21¼**	**21¾**	**22**	**22½ in.**

Sleeve length to underarm (C):					
45	45	46	46	46	47 cm
17¾	**17¾**	**18**	**18**	**18**	**18½ in.**

YARN

50 g balls of Nautical Cotton (Cotton), Red:

11	12	12	13	13	14

NEEDLES

Pair of 3¾ mm (US 5) knitting needles

Pair of 4½ mm (US 7) knitting needles

BUTTONS

10 small pearl buttons

TENSION

20 sts and 28 rows = 10 cm (4 in.) square measured over st st using 4½ mm (US 7) knitting needles.

BACK

Using 3¾ mm (US 5) needles, cast on 87 (91, 97, 101, 107, 111) sts. Knit 4 rows, ending with WS row.

Change to 4½ mm (US 7) needles.

Beg with a knit row, work in st st for 8 rows.

Next row (RS) (dec): K3, K2tog, knit to last 5 sts, K2tog tbl, K3.

Working all decs as set by last row, cont in st st, dec 1 st at each end of every foll 6th row until there are 79 (83, 89, 93, 99, 103) sts.

Work 15 rows even, ending with WS row.

Next row (RS) (inc): K3, M1, knit to last 3 sts, M1, K3.

Working all incs as set by last row, cont in st st, inc 1 st at each end of every foll 10th row until there are 87 (91, 97, 101, 107, 111) sts.

Work even until work measures 33 (33, 34, 34, 35, 35) cm [13 (13, 13½, 13½, 13¾, 13¾) in], ending with WS row.

Shape armholes

Cast off 5 (5, 5, 6, 6, 6) sts at beg of next 2 rows: 77 (81, 87, 89, 95, 99) sts.

Next row (RS) (dec): K3, K2tog, knit to last 5 sts, K2tog tbl, K3.

Next row (WS) (dec): P3, P2tog tbl, purl to last 5 sts, P2tog, P3.

Next row (RS) (dec): K3, K2tog, knit to last 5 sts, K2tog tbl, K3.

Working all decs as set by last row, dec 1 st at each end of next 1 (1, 3, 3, 5, 5) rows, then on every other row 1 (2, 2, 2, 2, 3) times, then on every foll 4th row until 67 (69, 71, 73, 75, 77) sts rem.

Work even until armhole measures 19 (20, 20, 21, 21, 22) cm [7½ (8, 8, 8¼, 8¼, 8¾) in.], ending with WS row.

Shape shoulders and back neck

Cast off 6 (6, 6, 6, 6, 7) sts at beg next 2 rows.

Cast off 6 (6, 6, 6, 6, 7) sts, knit until there are 9 (9, 10, 10, 11, 10) sts on RH needle and turn, place rem sts on a holder.

Work both sides of neck separately.

Cast off 4 sts, purl to end.

Cast off rem 5 (5, 6, 6, 7, 6) sts.

With RS facing, rejoin yarn to sts from holder and cast off centre 25 (27, 27, 29, 29, 29) sts, knit to end.

Complete to match first side, reversing shapings and working an extra row before beg of shoulder shaping.

LEFT FRONT

Using 3³/₄ mm (US 5) needles, cast on 45 (47, 50, 52, 55, 57) sts. Knit 4 rows, ending with WS row.

Change to 4¹/₂ mm (US 7) needles.

Beg with a knit row, work in st st for 8 rows.

Next row (RS) (dec): K3, K2tog, knit to end.

Working all decs as set by last row, cont in st st, dec 1 st at beg of every foll 6th row until there are 41 (43, 46, 48, 51, 53) sts.

Work 15 rows even, ending with WS row.

Next row (RS) (inc): K3, M1, knit to end.

Working all incs as set by last row, cont in st st, inc 1 st at beg of every foll 10th row until there are 45 (47, 50, 52, 55, 57) sts.

Work even until left front matches back to beg of armhole shaping, ending with WS row.

Shape armhole

Cast off 5 (5, 5, 6, 6, 6) sts beg next row: 40 (42, 45, 46, 49, 51) sts.

Work 1 row even.

Next row (RS) (dec): K3, K2tog, knit to end.

Next row (WS) (dec): Purl to last 5 sts, P2tog, P3.

Next row (RS) (dec): K3, K2tog, knit to end.

Working all decs as set by last row, dec 1 st at armhole edge of next 1 (1, 3, 3, 5, 5) rows, then on every other row 1 (2, 2, 2, 2, 3) times, then on every foll 4th row until 35 (36, 37, 38, 39, 40) sts rem.

Work even until you have worked 17 (19, 19, 19, 19, 21) rows fewer than on back to start of shoulder shaping, ending with RS row.

Shape neck

Cast off 10 sts at beg of next row.

Dec 1 st at neck edge on next 5 rows, then on every other row 2 (3, 3, 4, 4, 4) times, and then on foll 4th row 17 (17, 18, 18, 19, 20) sts rem.

Work even until left front matches back to start of shoulder shaping, ending with WS row.

Shape shoulder

Cast off 6 (6, 6, 6, 6, 7) sts at beg of next 2 RS rows.

Work 1 row even.

Cast off rem 5 (5, 6, 6, 7, 6) sts.

RIGHT FRONT

Using 3³/₄ mm (US 5) needles, cast on 45 (47, 50, 52, 55, 57) sts. Knit 4 rows, ending with WS row.

Change to 4¹/₂ mm (US 7) needles.

Beg with a knit row, work in st st for 8 rows.

Next row (RS) (dec): Knit to last 5 sts, K2tog tbl, K3.

Working all decs as set by last row, cont in st st, dec 1 st at end of every foll 6th row until there are 41 (43, 46, 48, 51, 53) sts.

Work 15 rows even, ending with WS row.

Next row (RS) (inc): Knit to last 3 sts, M1, K3.

Working all incs as set by last row, complete to match left front, reversing shaping and working an extra row before beg armhole, neck and shoulder shaping.

SLEEVES (work both the same)

Using 3³/₄ mm (US 5) needles, cast on 47 (49, 49, 51, 51, 53) sts. Knit 4 rows, ending with WS row.

Change to 4¹/₂ mm (US 7) needles.

Beg with a knit row, work in st st for 8 rows.

Next row (RS) (inc): K3, M1, knit to last 3 sts, M1, K3.
Working all incs as set by last row, cont in st st, inc 1 st at each
end of every foll 12th (12th, 12th, 12th, 10th, 12th) row to 63
(65, 59, 61, 71, 57) sts, then on every foll 10th (10th, 10th,
10th, 8th, 10th) row until there are 65 (67, 69, 71, 73, 75) sts.
Work even until sleeve measures 45 (45, 46, 46, 46, 47) cm
[17³/₄ (17³/₄, 18, 18, 18, 18¹/₂) in.], ending with WS row.

Shape sleevehead

Cast off 5 (5, 5, 6, 6, 6) sts at beg of next 2 rows: 55 (57, 59,
59, 61, 63) sts.

Dec 1 st at each end of next 3 (3, 5, 3, 5, 5) rows, then on
every other row 2 (2, 1, 2, 1, 1) times, and then on every foll
4th row until 35 (37, 37, 39, 39, 41) sts rem.

Work 1 row even.

Dec 1 st at each end of next row and then on every other row
0 (1, 1, 2, 2, 3) times, and then on every foll row until 27 sts rem.

Cast off 6 sts at beg of next 2 rows.

Cast off rem 15 sts.

FINISHING

Press as described on page 21.

Join both shoulder seams.

Make buttonhole band

With RS facing, starting at cast-on edge of right front and using
3³/₄ mm (US 5) needles, pick up and every 92 (92, 96, 96,
100, 100) sts to start of front neck shaping and knit 1 row,
ending with WS row.

Next row (RS) (buttonhole row): K2, *K2tog, YO, K8 (8, 9, 9,
9, 9), rep from * to last 10 (10, 6, 6, 10, 10) sts, K2tog, YO,
knit to end.

Cast off knitwise on WS.

Make button band

With RS facing and using 3³/₄ mm (US 5) needles, pick up and

knit 92 (92, 96, 96, 100, 100) sts along left front from start of
neck shaping to cast-on edge.

Knit 2 rows.

Cast off knitwise on WS.

Make neck edging

With RS facing and using 3³/₄ mm (US 5) needles, pick up and
knit 28 (29, 29, 29, 29, 30) sts to shoulder, 33 (35, 35, 37, 37,
37) sts across back neck, then 28 (29, 29, 29, 29, 30) sts
down left front neck: 89 (93, 93, 95, 95, 97) sts.

Knit 1 row, ending with WS row.

Next row (RS) (buttonhole row): K2, YO, K2tog tbl, knit to end.

Cast off knitwise on WS.

Join side and sleeve seams.

Match centre of cast off edge of sleeve to shoulder seam. Set
in sleeve, easing sleevehead into armhole.

Sew on buttons to correspond with buttonholes.

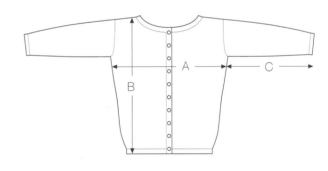

panel jacket

To fit bust size:					
81	86	91	97	102	107 cm
32	**34**	**36**	**38**	**40**	**42 in.**

Actual width at underarm (A):

91	97	101	107	111	117 cm
35³/₄	**38¹/₄**	**39³/₄**	**42**	**43³/₄**	**46 in.**

Finished length (B):

57	58	59	60	61	62 cm
22¹/₂	**22³/₄**	**23¹/₄**	**23¹/₂**	**24**	**24¹/₂ in.**

Sleeve length to underarm (C):

44	45	45	45	46	46 cm
17¹/₄	**17³/₄**	**17³/₄**	**17³/₄**	**18**	**18 in.**

YARN

50g balls of Nautical Cotton (Cotton), Natural:

12	13	14	14	15	16

NEEDLES

Pair of 3³/₄ mm (US 5) knitting needles
Pair of 4¹/₂ mm (US 7) knitting needles

BUTTONS

7 medium pearl buttons

TENSION

20 sts and 28 rows = 10 cm (4 in.) square measured over st st using (4¹/₂ mm (US 7) knitting needles.

This feminine jacket with its pretty scalloped edging is knitted in a moss-stitch stripe. The scallops are made separately and then knitted together.

BACK

Border panel blocks (make 6)

Using 3³/₄ mm (US 5) needles, cast on 18 (19, 20, 21, 22, 23) sts and work in moss st as folls:

Row 1 (RS): K0 (1, 0, 1, 0, 1), *P1, K1, rep from * to end.

Row 2: *K1, P1, rep from * to last 0 (1, 0, 1, 0, 1) sts, K0 (1, 0, 1, 0, 1).

Rep these 2 rows 14 times more, ending with a WS row.

Break yarn and place sts on a holder. Do not break yarn on final block.

Join blocks

With RS facing and using 3³/₄ mm (US 5) needles, join blocks as folls:

Next row (RS): (Work in moss st to last 3 sts, hold last 3 sts of current block in front of first 3 sts of next block and, taking 1 st from each needle tog, moss st 3) 5 times, work in moss st to end: 93 (99, 105, 111, 117, 123) sts.

Next row: Work in moss st, dec 2 (2, 4, 4, 6, 6) sts evenly across panels: 91 (97, 101, 107, 111, 117) sts.

Change to 4¹/₂ (US 7mm) needles and work in moss st stripe patt as folls:

Next row (RS): K15 (16, 16, 17, 17, 18), *P1, K14 (15, 16, 17, 18, 19), rep from * to last 16 (17, 17, 18, 18, 19) sts, P1, knit to end.

Next row: P14 (15, 15, 16, 16, 17), *K1, P1, K1, P12 (13, 14, 15, 16, 17), rep from * to last 17 (18, 18, 19, 19, 20) sts, K1, P1, K1, purl to end.

These 2 rows form moss st stripe patt and are rep throughout.

Work even in patt until back measures 29 (30, 30, 31, 31, 32) cm [11¹/₂ (11³/₄, 11³/₄, 12¹/₄, 12¹/₄, 12¹/₂) in.], from joining row ending with WS row.

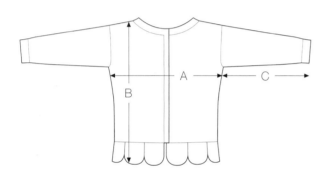

Shape armholes

Cast off 6 (6, 7, 7, 8, 8) sts at beg next 2 rows: 79 (85, 87, 93, 95, 101) sts.

Keeping in patt, dec 1 st at each end of next 3 (5, 5, 7, 7, 9) rows, then on every other row twice, and then on every foll 4th row until 67 (69, 71, 73, 75, 77) sts rem.

Work even until armhole measures 20 (20, 21, 21, 22, 22) cm [8 (8, 8¼, 8¼, 8¾, 8¾) in.], ending with RS facing for next row.

Shape shoulders and back neck

Keeping in patt, cast off 8 (8, 9, 9, 9, 10) sts at beg of next row, work in patt until there are 13 (13, 13, 13, 14, 14) sts on right needle and turn, place rem sts on a holder.

Work both sides of neck separately.

Cast off 4 sts, work in patt to end.

Cast off rem 9 (9, 9, 9, 10, 10) sts.

With RS facing rejoin yarn to sts from holder, and cast off centre 25 (27, 27, 29, 29, 29) sts, work in patt to end.

Complete to match first side, reversing shaping and working an extra row before beg of shoulder shaping.

LEFT FRONT

Border panel blocks (make 3)

Using 3¾ mm (US 5) needles, cast on 18 (19, 20, 21, 22, 23) sts.

Row 1 (RS): K0 (1, 0, 1, 0, 1), *P1, K1, rep from * to end.

Row 2: *K1, P1, rep from * to last 0 (1, 0, 1, 0, 1) sts, K0 (1, 0, 1, 0, 1).

Rep these 2 rows 14 times more, ending with a WS row.

Break yarn and place sts on a holder. Do not break yarn on final block.

Join blocks

With RS facing and using 3¾ mm (US 5) needles, join blocks as folls:

Next row (RS): (Work in moss st to last 3 sts, hold last 3 sts of current block in front of first 3 sts of next block and, taking 1 st

from each needle tog, moss st 3) twice, work in moss st to end: 48 (51, 54, 57, 60, 63) sts.

Next row: Work in moss st to end, dec 2 (2, 3, 3, 4, 4) sts evenly across panels: 46 (49, 51, 54, 56, 59) sts.

Change to 4¹/₂ mm (US 7) needles and cont in moss st stripe patt as folls:

Next row (RS): K15 (16, 16, 17, 17, 18), *P1, K14 (15, 16, 17, 18, 19), rep from * to last st, P1.

Next row: P1, K1, *P12 (13, 14, 15, 16, 17), K1, P1, K1, rep from * to last 14 (15, 15, 16, 16, 17) sts, purl to end.

These 2 rows form moss st stripe patt and are rep throughout.

Work even until left front matches back to beg of armhole shaping, ending with WS row.

Shape armhole

Cast off 6 (6, 7, 7, 8, 8) sts at beg next row: 40 (43, 44, 47, 48, 51) sts.

Work 1 row even.

Keeping in patt, dec 1 st at armhole edge of next 3 (5, 5, 7, 7, 9) rows, then on every other row twice, then on every foll 4th row until 34 (35, 36, 37, 38, 39) sts rem.

Work even until you have worked 15 (15, 15, 17, 17, 17) rows fewer than on back to start of shoulder shaping, ending with RS row.

Shape neck

Next row (WS): Cast off 9 (10, 10, 10, 10, 10) sts at beg of next row: 25 (25, 26, 27, 28, 29) sts.

Dec 1 st at neck edge on next 5 rows, then on every other row 2 (2, 2, 3, 3, 3) times, and then on foll 4th row. 17 (17, 18, 18, 19, 20) sts.

Work even until left front matches back to beg of shoulder shaping, ending with WS row.

Shape shoulder

Cast off 8 (8, 9, 9, 9, 10) sts at beg of next row.

Work 1 row even.

Cast off rem 9 (9, 9, 9, 10, 10) sts.

RIGHT FRONT

Border panel blocks (make 3)

Using 3³/₄ mm (US 5) needles, cast on 18 (19, 20, 21, 22, 23) sts

Row 1 (RS): *P1, K1, rep from * to last 0 (1, 0, 1, 0, 1) sts, P0 (1, 0, 1, 0, 1).

Row 2: P0 (1, 0, 1, 0, 1), *K1, P1, rep from * to end.

Rep these 2 rows 14 times more, ending with a WS row.

Break yarn and place sts on a holder. Do not break yarn on final block.

Join blocks

With RS facing and using 3³/₄ mm (US 5) needles, join blocks as folls:

Next row (RS): (Work in moss st to last 3 sts, hold last 3 sts of current block in front of first 3 sts of next block and, taking 1 st from each needle tog, moss st 3) twice, work in moss st to end: 48 (51, 54, 57, 60, 63) sts.

Next row: Work in moss st, dec 2 (2, 3, 3, 4, 4) sts evenly across panels: 46 (49, 51, 54, 56, 59) sts.

Change to 4¹/₂ mm (US 7) needles and cont in moss st stripe patt as folls:

Next row (RS): *P1, K14 (15, 16, 17, 18, 19), rep from * to last 16 (17, 17, 18, 18, 19) sts, P1, knit to end.

Next row: P14 (15, 15, 16, 16, 17), *K1, P1, K1, P12 (13, 14, 15, 16, 17), rep from * to last 2 sts, K1, P1.

These 2 rows form moss st stripe patt and are rep throughout.

Cont in patt, complete to match left front, reversing shaping and working an extra row before beg armhole, neck and shoulder shaping.

SLEEVES (work both the same)

Using 3³/₄ mm (US 5) needles, cast on 49 (49, 51, 51, 51, 53) sts. Work in 12 rows of moss st as folls:

All rows: K1 (0, 0, 1, 0, 0), *P1, K1, rep from to last 0 (1, 1, 0, 1, 1) sts, P0 (1, 1, 0, 1, 1).

Change to 4¹/₂ mm (US 7) needles and work in moss st stripe

patt as folls:

Next row (RS): K9 (8, 8, 7, 6, 6), *P1, K14 (15, 16, 17, 18, 19), rep from * to last 10 (9, 9, 8, 7, 7) sts, P1, knit to end.

Next row: P8 (7, 7, 6, 5, 5), *K1, P1, K1, P12 (13, 14, 15, 16, 17), rep from * to last 11 (10, 10, 9, 8, 8) sts, K1, P1, K1, purl to end.

These 2 rows set moss st stripe patt.

Cont in patt, inc 1 st at each end of next and every foll 14th (12th, 12th, 10th, 10th, 10th) row to 55 (61, 63, 73, 65, 67) sts, then on every foll 12th (10th, 10th, 0, 8th, 8th) row until there are 67 (69, 71, 73, 75, 77) sts, working inc sts in patt. Work even until sleeve measures 44 (45, 45, 45, 46, 46) cm [17¼ (17¾, 17¾, 17¾, 18, 18) in.], ending with WS row.

Shape sleevehead

Keeping patt correct, cast off 6 (6, 7, 7, 8, 8) sts at beg of next 2 rows: 55 (57, 57, 59, 59, 61) sts.

Dec 1 st at each end of next 5 rows, then on foll alt row, then on every foll 4th row until 33 (35, 35, 37, 37, 39) sts rem.

Work 1 row even.

Dec 1 st at each end of next row and on every other row 1 (1, 2, 2, 3, 3) times, and then on 3 foll rows.

Cast off 5 sts at beg of next 2 rows.

Cast off rem 13 (15, 13, 15, 13, 15) sts.

FINISHING

Press as described on page 21.

Join shoulder seams.

Neck edging

With RS facing and using 3¾ mm (US 5) needles, PU 24 (25, 25, 26, 26, 26) sts to shoulder, 33 (35, 35, 37, 37, 37) sts across back neck, then 24 (25, 25, 26, 26, 26) sts down left front neck: 81 (85, 85, 89, 89, 89) sts.

Work 4 rows in moss st as folls:

All rows: *K1, P1, rep from to last st, K1.

Cast off knitwise on WS.

Make buttonhole band

With RS facing and starting at cast-on edge of right front and using 3¾ mm (US 5) needles, pick up and knit 101 (101, 101, 107, 107, 107) sts to neck shaping and work 1 row in moss st as given for neck edging, ending with WS row.

Next row (RS) (buttonhole row): Working in moss st, work 2 sts, *work 2tog, YO, work 13 (13, 13, 14, 14, 14) sts, rep from * to last 9 sts, work 2tog, YO, work in moss st to end.

Work a further 2 rows in moss st.

Cast off knitwise on WS.

Make button band

With RS facing and using 3¾ mm (US 5) needles, pick up and knit 101 (101, 101, 107, 107, 107) sts along left front from start of neck shaping to cast-on edge. Work 4 rows in moss st as given for neck edging.

Cast off knitwise on WS.

Join side and sleeve seams.

Match centre of cast off edge of sleeve to shoulder seam. Set in sleeve, easing sleevehead into armhole.

Sew on buttons to correspond with buttonholes.

sloppy joe

To fit bust size:					
81	86	91	97	102	107 cm
32	**34**	**36**	**38**	**40**	**42 in.**

Actual width at underarm (A):

96	102	106	112	116	122 cm
37³/₄	**40¹/₄**	**41³/₄**	**44**	**45³/₄**	**48 in.**

Finished length (B):

58	59	60	61	62	63 cm
22³/₄	**23¹/₄**	**23¹/₂**	**24**	**24¹/₂**	**24³/₄ in.**

Sleeve length to underarm (C):

44	45	45	45	46	46 cm
17¹/₄	**17³/₄**	**17³/₄**	**17³/₄**	**18**	**18 in.**

YARN

50 g balls of Nautical Cotton (Cotton), Rose:

12	13	13	14	15	15

NEEDLES

Pair of 3³/₄ mm (US 5) knitting needles
Pair of 4 mm (US 6) knitting needles
Pair of 4¹/₂ mm (US 7) knitting needles

TENSION

20 sts and 28 rows = 10 cm (4 in.) square measured over rib patt using 4¹/₂ mm (US 7) knitting needles.

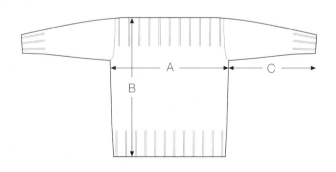

Roomy and just perfect for lounging around, this pretty jumper is easy to knit. It is also very feminine with its soft colour and rib stripes.

BACK AND FRONT (work both the same)

Using 4 mm (US 6) needles, cast on 96 (102, 106, 112, 116, 122) sts and work in rib as folls:

Row 1 (RS): K0 (0, 0, 0, 1, 0), P1 (0, 2, 1, 2, 2), *K2, P2, rep from * to last 3 (2, 4, 3, 5, 4) sts, K2, P1 (0, 2, 1, 2, 2), K0 (0, 0, 0, 1, 0).

Row 2: P0 (0, 0, 0, 1, 0), K1 (0, 2, 1, 2, 2), *P2, K2, rep from * to last 3 (2, 4, 3, 5, 4) sts, P2, K1 (0, 2, 1, 2, 2), P0 (0, 0, 0, 1, 0).

Rep these 2 rows 11 times more, ending with WS row.

Change to 4¹/₂ mm (US 7) needles and work in rib patt as folls:

Next row (RS): P1 (0, 0, 0, 0, 0), K10 (2, 4, 7, 9, 0), *P2, K10, rep from * to last 1 (4, 6, 9, 11, 2) sts, P1 (2, 2, 2, 2, 2), K0 (2, 4, 7, 9, 0).

Next row: K1 (0, 0, 0, 0, 0), P10 (2, 4, 7, 9, 0), *K2, P10, rep from * to last 1 (4, 6, 9, 11, 2) sts, K1 (2, 2, 2, 2, 2), P0 (2, 4, 7, 9, 0).

These 2 rows form rib patt.

Cont in patt, work even until back measures 38 (39, 39, 40, 40, 41) cm [15 (15¹/₄, 15¹/₄, 15³/₄, 15³/₄, 16¹/₄) in], ending with WS row.

Shape armholes

Cast off 6 (6, 7, 7, 8, 8) sts at beg of next 2 rows: 84 (90, 92, 98, 100, 106) sts.

Dec 1 st at each end of next 5 (7, 7, 9, 9, 11) rows, then on every other row twice and then on every foll 4th row until 68 (70, 72, 74, 76, 78) sts rem.

Work without further shaping until armhole measures 3 (13, 14, 14, 15, 15) cm [5 (5, 5¹/₂, 5¹/₂, 6, 5) in.], ending with WS row.

Next row (RS): K1 (0, 0, 0, 1, 0), P2 (0, 1, 2, 2, 0), *K2, P2, rep from * to last 1 (2, 3, 0, 1, 2) sts, K1 (2, 2, 0, 1, 2), P0 (0, 1, 0, 0, 0).

Next row: P1 (0, 0, 0, 1, 0), K2 (0, 1, 2, 2, 0), *P2, K2, rep from * to last 1 (2, 3, 0, 1, 2) sts, P1 (2, 2, 0, 1, 2), K0 (0, 1, 0, 0, 0).

These 2 rows form rib.

Work even in rib until armhole measures 20 (20, 21, 21, 22, 22) cm [8 (8, 8¼, 8¼, 8¾, 8¾) in.], ending with RS row.

Cast off in rib on WS.

SLEEVES (work both the same)

Using 3¾ mm (US 5) needles, cast on 50 (50, 52, 52, 54, 54) sts and work in rib as folls:

Row 1 (RS): K0 (0, 1, 1, 0, 0), P2 (2, 2, 2, 0, 0), *K2, P2, rep from * to last 0 (0, 1, 1, 2, 2) sts, K0 (0, 1, 1, 2, 2).

Row 2: P0 (0, 1, 1, 0, 0), K2 (2, 2, 2, 0, 0), *P2, K2, rep from * to last 0 (0, 1, 1, 2, 2) sts, P0 (0, 1, 1, 2, 2).

Rep these 2 rows 11 times more, ending with WS row.

Change to 4½ mm (US 7) needles and work in rib patt as folls:

Next row (RS): K0 (0, 1, 1, 2, 2), *P2, K10, rep from * to last 2 (2, 3, 3, 4, 4) sts, P2, K0 (0, 1, 1, 2, 2).

Next row: P0 (0, 1, 1, 2, 2), *K2, P10, rep from * to last 2 (2, 3, 3, 4, 4) sts, K2, P0 (0, 1, 1, 2, 2).

These 2 rows form rib patt.

Inc 1 st at each end of 5th (5th, 5th, next, next, next) and every foll 10th (10th, 8th, 8th, 8th, 8th) row to 68 (68, 58, 60, 68, 70) sts, then on every foll 0 (12th, 10th, 10th, 10th, 10th) row until there are 68 (70, 72, 74, 76, 78) sts, taking inc sts into patt.

Work even until sleeve measures 44 (45, 45, 45, 46, 46) cm [17¼ (17¾, 17¾, 17¾, 18, 18) in.], ending with WS row.

Shape sleevehead

Keeping in patt, cast off 6 (6, 7, 7, 8, 8) sts at beg of next 2 rows: 56 (58, 58, 60, 60, 62) sts.

Dec 1 st at each end of next 5 rows, then on foll alt row, then on every foll 4th row until 34 (36, 36, 38, 38, 40) sts rem.

Work 1 row even.

Dec 1 st at each end of next row and then on every other row 2 (2, 3, 3, 4, 4) times, and then on foll row.

Cast off 5 (6, 5, 6, 5, 6) sts at beg of next 2 rows.

Cast off rem 16 sts.

FINISHING

Press as described on page 21.

Join front and back cast off edges together for first 1 in. (3 cm) to form shoulder seam.

Join side and sleeve seams, leaving side seams open for first 24 rows to form vents.

Match centre of cast off edge of sleeve to shoulder seam.

Set in sleeve, easing sleevehead into armhole.

relaxed cardigan

This casual cardigan is knit in rib so it stretches and clings. It is fastened with a single button, allowing the front to flare open gently and echo the V-neck.

To fit bust size:

81	86	91	97	102	107 cm
32	**34**	**36**	**38**	**40**	**42 in.**

Actual width at underarm (A):

87	91	97	101	107	111 cm
34¼	**36**	**38**	**39¾**	**42**	**43¾ in.**

Finished length (B):

52	53	54	55	56	57 cm
20½	**21**	**21¼**	**21¾**	**22**	**22½ in.**

Sleeve length to underarm (C):

44	45	45	45	46	46 cm
17½	**17¾**	**17¾**	**17¾**	**18**	**18 in.**

YARN
50 g balls of Fauve (Nylon), #14 Purple:

13	13	14	14	15	15

NEEDLES
Pair of 6 mm (US 10) knitting needles
Pair of 6½ mm (US 10½) knitting needles
6 mm (US 10) circular needle

BUTTON
1 medium button

TENSION
20 sts and 28 rows = 10 cm (4 in.) square measured over st st using 6½ mm (US 10½) knitting needles.

BACK
Using 6 mm (US 10) needles, cast on 87 (91, 97, 101, 107, 111) sts. Knit 4 rows, ending with WS row.

Change to 6½ mm (US 10½) needles and work in rib patt as folls:

Next row (RS): K1 (3, 0, 2, 5, 1), *P1, K5, rep from * to last 2 (4, 1, 3, 6, 2) sts, P1, K1 (3, 0, 2, 5, 1).

Next row: Purl.

These 2 rows form patt.

Cont in patt as set, dec 1 st at each end of 7th and every foll 6th row until 79 (83, 89, 93, 99, 103) sts rem.

Work 15 rows even, ending with WS row.

Inc 1 st at each end of next and every foll 12th row until there are 87 (91 ,97, 101, 107, 111) sts, working inc sts in patt.

Work even until work measures 33 (34, 34, 35, 35, 36) cm [13 (13½, 13½, 13¾, 13¾, 14¼)], ending with WS row.

Shape armholes

Keeping in patt, cast off 5 (6, 6, 7, 7, 8) sts at beg of next 2 rows: 77 (79, 85, 87, 93, 95) sts.

Dec 1 st at each end of next 3 (3, 5, 5, 7, 7) rows, then on every other row until 67 (69, 71, 73, 75, 77) sts rem.

Work even until armhole measures 19 (19, 20, 20, 21, 21) cm, [7½ (7½, 8, 8, 8¼, 8¼) in.], ending with WS row.

Shape shoulders and back neck

Cast off 6 (6, 6, 6, 6, 7) sts at beg of next 2 rows: 55 (57, 59, 61, 63, 63) sts.

Cast off 6 (6, 6, 6, 6, 7) sts, work in patt until there are 8 (9, 9, 10, 10, 9) sts on RH needle and turn, place rem sts on a holder.

Work both sides of neck separately.

Cast off 3 sts, purl to end.

Cast off rem 5 (6, 6, 7, 7, 6) sts.

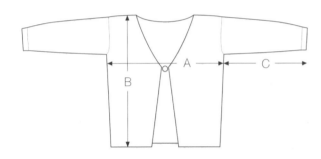

With RS facing, rejoin yarn to sts from holder, and cast off centre 27 (27, 29, 29, 31, 31) sts, work in patt to end.
Complete to match first side, reversing shaping and working an extra row before start of shoulder shaping.

LEFT FRONT

Using 6 mm (US 10) needles, cast off 44 (46, 49, 51, 54, 56) sts. Knit 4 rows, ending with WS row.
Change to 6¹/₂ mm (US 10¹/₂) needles and work in patt as folls:
Next row (RS): K1 (3, 0, 2, 5, 1), *P1, K5, rep from * to last st, K1.
Next row: Purl.
These 2 rows form patt.
Cont in patt as set, dec 1 st at beg of 7th and every foll 6th row until 40 (42, 45, 47, 50, 52) sts rem.
Work 15 rows, ending with WS row.
Inc 1 st at beg of next and every foll 12th row until there are 44 (46, 49, 51, 54, 56) sts, working inc sts in patt.
Work even until left front matches back to beg of armhole shaping, ending with WS row.
Shape armhole and front neck
Cast off 5 (6, 6, 7, 7, 8) sts at beg and dec 1 st at end of next row: 38 (39, 42, 43, 46, 47) sts.
Work 1 row even.
Dec 1 st at armhole edge of next 3 (3, 5, 5, 7, 7) rows, then on every other twice **and at the same time**, dec 1 st at neck edge on next row and then every other row until 29 (30, 30, 31, 31, 32) sts rem.
Work 1 row even, ending with WS row.
Dec 1 st at neck edge only on next row then on every other row twice, and then on every foll 4th row until 17 (18, 18, 19, 19, 20) sts rem.
Work even until left front matches back to start of shoulder shaping, ending with WS row.

Shape shoulder

Cast off 6 (6, 6, 6, 6, 7) sts at beg of next 2 RS rows.

Work 1 row even.

Cast off rem 5 (6, 6, 7, 7, 6) sts.

RIGHT FRONT

Using 6 mm (US 10) needles, cast on 44 (46, 49, 51, 54, 56) sts. Knit 4 rows, ending with WS row.

Change to 6 1/2 mm (US 10 1/2) needles and work in patt as folls:

Next row (RS): K6, *P1, K5, rep from * to last 2 (4, 1, 3, 6, 2) sts, P1, K1 (3, 0, 2, 5, 1).

Next row: Purl.

These 2 rows form patt.

Cont in patt as set, complete to match left front, reversing shaping and working an extra row before start of armhole, neck and shoulder shaping.

SLEEVES (work both the same)

Using 6 mm (US 10) needles, cast on 47 (49, 49, 51, 51, 53) sts. Knit 4 rows, ending with WS row.

Change to 6 1/2 mm (US 10 1/2) needles and work in patt as folls:

Next row (RS): K5 (0, 0, 1, 1, 2), *P1, K5, rep from * to last 6 (1, 1, 2, 2, 3) sts, P1, K5 (0, 0, 1, 1, 2).

Next row: Purl.

These 2 rows form patt.

Cont in patt, inc 1 st at each end of 7th row and every foll 12th (12th, 12th, 12th, 10th, 10th) row to 53 (55, 53, 55, 71, 73) sts, then on every foll 10th (10th, 10th, 10th, 8th, 8th) row until there are 67 (69, 71, 73, 75, 77) sts, working inc sts in patt.

Work even until sleeve measures 44 (45, 45, 45, 46, 46) cm, [17 1/2 (17 3/4, 17 3/4, 17 3/4, 18, 18) in.], ending with RS facing for next row.

Shape sleevehead

Keeping in patt, cast off 5 (6, 6, 7, 7, 8) sts at beg of next 2 rows: 57 (57, 59, 59, 61, 61) sts.

Dec 1 st at each end of next 3 rows, then on every other row twice, and then on every foll 4th row until 37 (37, 37, 37, 39, 39) sts rem.

Work 1 row even.

Dec 1 st at each end of next row and 1 (1, 0, 0, 1, 1) foll alt rows, then on 3 foll rows, ending with WS row.

Cast off 5 (5, 6, 6, 6, 6) sts at beg of next 2 rows.

Cast off rem 17 sts.

FINISHING

Press as described on page 21.

Join shoulder seams.

Make edgings

With RS facing and using 6 mm (US 10) circular needle, starting at right front cast on edge, pick up and knit 66 (68, 68, 70, 70, 72) sts up right front opening edge to start of neck shaping, 48 (48, 50, 50, 52, 52) sts up right front neck, 33 (33, 35, 35, 37, 37) sts from back, 48 (48, 50, 50, 52, 52) sts down left front neck, then 66 (68, 68, 70, 70, 72) sts down left front to cast off edge: 261 (265, 271, 275, 281, 285) sts.

Knit 2 rows.

Cast off knitwise on WS.

Join side and sleeve seams.

Match centre of cast off edge to shoulder seam. Set in sleeve, easing sleevehead into armhole.

Make button loop

Using 6 mm (US 10) needles, cast on 10 sts, cast off 10 sts. Sew lioop to right front at start of front slope shaping. Sew on button at corresponding edge of left front.

aran

longline jacket

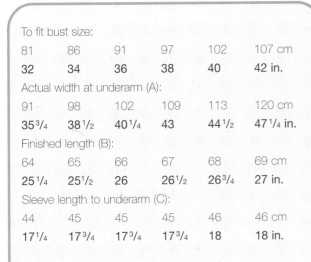

To fit bust size:

81	86	91	97	102	107 cm
32	**34**	**36**	**38**	**40**	**42 in.**

Actual width at underarm (A):

91	98	102	109	113	120 cm
35³/4	**38¹/2**	**40¹/4**	**43**	**44¹/2**	**47¹/4 in.**

Finished length (B):

64	65	66	67	68	69 cm
25¹/4	**25¹/2**	**26**	**26¹/2**	**26³/4**	**27 in.**

Sleeve length to underarm (C):

44	45	45	45	46	46 cm
17¹/4	**17³/4**	**17³/4**	**17³/4**	**18**	**18 in.**

YARN

50 g balls of Kashmir Aran (Merino/cashmere/microfiber), # 8 Olive:

18	18	19	19	20	20

NEEDLES

Pair of 4¹/2 mm (US 7) knitting needles
Pair of 5 mm (US 8) knitting needles
4¹/2 mm (US 7) circular needle

BUTTONS

8 large buttons

GAUGE

18 sts and 24 rows = 10 cm (4 in.) square measured over st st using 5 mm (US 8) knitting needles.

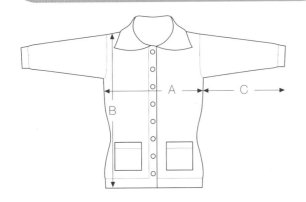

Knit in a luxurious cashmere blend, this long jacket is slim and shapely, clinging to feminine curves in a very flattering way.

BACK

Using 4¹/2 mm (US 7) needles, cast on 82 (88, 92, 98, 102, 108) sts.

Beg with a knit row, work 8 rows in garter st, ending with WS row.

Change to 5 mm (US 8) needles and, beg with a knit row, work in st st, dec 1 st at each end of 19th row and every foll 6th row until 74 (80, 84, 90, 94, 100) sts rem.

Work 13 (15, 15, 17, 17, 19) rows even, ending with WS row.

Inc 1 st at each end of next row and every foll 12th row until there are 82 (88, 92, 98, 102, 108) sts.

Work even until work measures 44 (45, 45, 46, 46, 47) cm [17¹/4 (17³/4, 17³/4, 18, 18, 18¹/2) in.], ending with WS row.

Shape armholes

Cast off 6 (6, 7, 7, 8, 8) sts at beg next 2 rows: 70 (76, 78, 84, 86, 92) sts.

Dec 1 st at each end of next 3 (5, 5, 7, 7, 9) rows, then on every other row twice: 60 (62, 64, 66, 68, 70) sts.

Work even until armhole measures 20 (20, 21, 21, 22, 22) cm, [8 (8, 8¹/4, 8¹/4, 8³/4, 8³/4) in], ending with WS row.

Shape shoulders and back neck

Cast off 5 (5, 6, 6, 6, 6) sts at beg of next 2 rows: 50 (52, 52, 54, 56, 58) sts.

Next row (RS): Cast off 5 (5, 6, 6, 6, 6) sts at beg of next row, knit until there are 8 (9, 8, 8, 9, 10) sts on RH needle and turn, place rem sts on a holder.

Work both sides of neck separately.

Casts off 3 sts, purl to end.

Cast off rem 5 (6, 5, 5, 6, 7) sts.

With RS facing, rejoin yarn to sts from holder, and cast off centre 24 (24, 24, 26, 26, 26) sts, knit to end.

Complete to match first side, reversing shaping and working an extra row, before beg of shoulder shaping.

POCKET LININGS (make 2)

Using 5 mm (US 8) needles, cast on 20 sts. Beg with a knit row, work 24 rows in st st.

Break yarn and place sts on a holder.

LEFT FRONT

Using 4¹/₂mm (US 7) needles, cast on 41 (44, 46, 49, 51, 54) sts.

Beg with a knit row, work 8 rows in garter st, ending with WS row.

Change to 5 mm (US 8) needles and, beg with a knit row, work in st st, dec 1 st at beg of 19th row and foll 6th row.

Work 5 rows even, ending with WS row.

Place pocket

Next row (RS): K2tog, K9 (12, 14, 17, 19, 22), slip next 20 sts to holder, knit across 20 sts from first pocket lining, knit to end.

Work 5 rows even.

Dec 1 st at beg of next row: 37 (40, 42, 45, 47, 50) sts.

Work 13 (15, 15, 17, 17, 19) rows even, ending with RS facing for next row.

Inc 1 st at beg of next row and every foll 12th row until there are 41 (44, 46, 49, 51, 54) sts.

Work without further shaping until left front measures the same as back to beg of armhole shaping, ending with WS row.

Shape armhole

Cast off 6 (6, 7, 7, 8, 8) sts at beg of next row: 35 (38, 39, 42, 43, 46) sts.

Work 1 row even.

Dec 1 st at armhole edge of next 3 (5, 5, 7, 7, 9) rows, then on every other row twice: 30 (31, 32, 33, 34, 35) sts.

Work even until left front is 15 (15, 15, 17, 17, 17) rows shorter than back to start of shoulder shaping, ending with RS row.

Shape neck

Cast off 7 sts at beg of next row.

Dec 1 st at neck edge on next 5 rows, then on every other row 2 (2, 2, 3, 3, 3) times, and then on every foll 4th row until 15 (16, 17, 17, 18, 19) sts rem.

Work even until left front matches back to beg of shoulder shaping, ending with WS row.

Shape shoulder

Cast off 5 (5, 6, 6, 6, 6) sts at beg of next 2 RS rows.

Work 1 row even.

Cast off rem 5 (6, 5, 5, 6, 7) sts.

RIGHT FRONT

Using 4¹/₂mm (US 7) needles, cast on 41 (44, 46, 49, 51, 54) sts.

Beg with a knit row, work 8 rows in garter st, ending with WS row.

Change to 5 mm (US 8) needles and, beg with a knit row, work in st st, dec 1 st at end of 19th row and foll 6th row.

Work 5 rows even, ending with WS row.

Place pocket

Next row (RS): K8, slip next 20 sts to holder, knit across 20 sts from pocket lining, knit to last 2 sts, K2tog.

Work 5 rows even.

Dec 1 st at end of next row: 37 (40, 42, 45, 47, 50) sts.

Work 13 rows even, ending with WS row.

Inc 1 st at end of next row and every foll 12th row until there are 41 (44, 46, 49, 51, 54) sts.

Complete to match left front, reversing shaping and working an extra row before start of armhole, neck, and shoulder shaping.

SLEEVES (work both the same)

Using 4¹/₂mm (US 7) needles, cast on 42 (44, 44, 46, 46, 46) sts.

Beg with a knit row, work 8 rows in garter st, ending with WS row.

Change to 5 mm (US 8) needles and, beg with a knit row, work in st st, inc 1 st at each end of 5th and every foll 10th (12th, 10th, 10th, 10th, 8th) row to 60 (48, 56, 58, 54, 68) sts, then on every foll 0 (10th, 8th, 8th, 8th, 6th) row until there are 60 (62, 64, 66, 68, 70) sts.

Work even until sleeve measures 44 (45, 45, 45, 46, 46) cm 17¹/₄ (17³/₄, 17³/₄, 17³/₄, 18, 18) in.], ending with WS row.

Shape sleevehead

Cast on 6 (6, 7, 7, 8, 8) sts at beg next 2 rows: 48 (50, 50, 52, 52, 54) sts.

Dec 1 st at each end of next 3 rows, then on every other row once, and then on every foll 4th row until 32 (34, 34, 36, 36, 38) sts rem.

Work 1 row even.

Dec 1 st at each end of next row and on every other row 1 (1, 2, 2, 3, 3) times, and then on next 5 rows.

Cast off rem 18 (20, 18, 20, 18, 20) sts.

FINISHING

Press as described on page 21.

Join shoulder seams.

Make button band

With RS facing and using 4¹/₂ mm (US 7) needles, pick up and knit 113 sts along left front opening edge between beg of neck shaping and cast-on edge.

Knit 6 rows.

Cast off knitwise on WS.

Make buttonhole band

With RS facing and using 4¹/₂ mm (US 7) needles, pick up and knit 113 sts along right front opening edge between cast-on edge and beg of neck shaping.

Knit 3 rows, ending with WS row.

Next row (RS) (buttonhole row): K4, *YO, K2tog tbl, K13, rep from * to last 4 sts, YO, K2tog tbl, K2.

Knit 2 rows.

Cast off knitwise on WS.

Make collar

With RS facing and using 4¹/₂ mm (US 7) needles, starting and ending halfway across front bands, pick up and knit 28 (28, 28, 30, 30, 30) sts up right front neck, 30 (30, 30, 32, 32, 32) sts from back, and 28 (28, 28, 30, 30, 30) sts down left front neck: 86 (86, 86, 92, 92, 92) sts.

Work until garter st until collar measures 14 cm (5¹/₂ in).

Cast off.

Make pocket tops (both alike)

With RS facing and using 4¹/₂ mm (US 7) needles, rejoin yarn to sts from holder and knit 5 rows.

Cast off knitwise on WS.

Join side and sleeve seams.

Match centre of cast off edge to shoulder seam.

Set in sleeve, easing sleevehead into armhole.

BELT

Using 4¹/₂ mm (US 7) circular needle, cast on 330 sts and, beg with a RS row, work 19 rows in garter st.

Cast off knitwise on WS.

Make belt loops

Using 4½ mm (US 7) needles, cast on 15 sts.

Cast off all sts. Attach to side seam at waist level.

cable-edged tunic

To fit bust size:					
81	86	91	97	102	107 cm
32	**34**	**36**	**38**	**40**	**42 in.**

Actual width at underarm (A):

91	98	102	109	113	120 cm
35³/₄	38¹/₂	40¹/₄	43	44¹/₂	47¹/₄ in.

Finished length (B):

55	56	57	58	59	60 cm
21³/₄	22	22¹/₂	22³/₄	23¹/₄	23¹/₂ in.

Sleeve length to underarm C:

44	45	45	45	46	46 cm
17¹/₄	17³/₄	17³/₄	17³/₄	18	18 in.

YARN

50g balls of Kashmir Aran (Merino/cashmere/microfibre), #10 Purple:

13	14	14	15	15	16

NEEDLES

Pair of 4¹/₂ mm (US 7) knitting needles
Pair of 5 mm (US 8) knitting needles
Cable needle

TENSION

18 sts and 24 rows = 10 cm (4 in.) square measured over st st using 5 mm (US 8) knitting needles.

A band of cable forms an unusual edging on this elegant tunic. Wear it as a stylish top with an evening skirt or velvet trousers.

BACK

Using 5 mm (US 8) needles, cast on 82 (88, 92, 98, 102, 108) sts.

Beg with a knit row, work in st st until work measures 29 (30, 30, 31, 31, 32) cm [11¹/₂ (11³/₄, 11³/₄, 12¹/₄, 12¹/₄, 12¹/₂) in.], ending with WS row.

Shape armholes

Cast off 6 (6, 7, 7, 8, 8) sts at beg next 2 rows: 70 (76, 78, 84, 86, 92) sts.

Dec 1 st at each end of next 3 (5, 5, 7, 7, 9) rows, then on every other row twice: 60 (62, 64, 66, 68, 70) sts.

Work even until armhole measures 20 (20, 21, 21, 22, 22) cm [8 (8, 8¹/₄, 8¹/₄, 8³/₄, 8³/₄) in], ending with WS row.

Shape shoulders and back neck

Cast off 5 (5, 6, 6, 6, 6) sts at beg of next 2 rows: 50 (52, 52, 54, 56, 58) sts.

Next row (RS): Cast off 5 (5, 6, 6, 6, 6) sts at beg of next row, knit until there are 8 (9, 8, 8, 9, 10) sts on RH and turn, place rem sts on a holder.

Work both sides of neck separately.

Cast off 3 sts, purl to end.

Cast off rem 5 (6, 5, 5, 6, 7) sts.

With RS facing, rejoin yarn to sts from holder, and cast off centre 24 (24, 24, 26, 26, 26) sts, knit to end.

Complete to match first side, reversing shaping and working an extra row before beg of shoulder shaping.

FRONT

Work as for back until you have worked 14 (14, 14, 16, 16, 16) rows fewer than on back to start of shoulder shaping, ending with WS row.

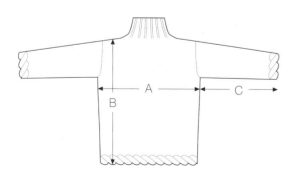

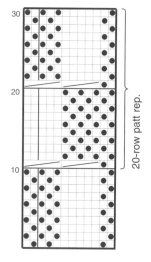

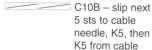

Key

☐ K on RS, P on WS

▣ P on RS, K on WS

C10B – slip next 5 sts to cable needle, K5, then K5 from cable needle.

Shape neck

Next row (RS): K22 (23, 24, 25, 26, 27) and turn, place rem sts on a holder.

Dec 1 st at neck edge on next 4 rows, then on every other row 2 (2, 2, 3, 3, 3) times, and then on every foll 4th row until 15 (16, 17, 17, 18, 19) sts rem.

Work even until front matches back to beg of shoulder shaping, ending with WS row.

Shape shoulder

Cast off 5 (5, 6, 6, 6, 6) sts at beg of next 2 RS rows.

Work 1 row even.

Cast off rem 5 (6, 5, 5, 6, 7) sts.

With RS facing, rejoin yarn to sts from holder, and cast off centre 16 sts, knit to end.

Complete to match first side, reversing shaping.

SLEEVES (work both the same)

Using 5 mm (US 8) needles, cast off 42 (44, 44, 46, 46, 46) sts.

Beg with a knit row, work in st st, inc 1 st at each end of 11th and every foll 10th (10th, 8th, 8th, 8th, 8th) row to 50 (54, 64, 66, 66, 60) sts, then on every foll 8th (8th, 0, 0, 6th, 6th) row until there are 60 (62, 64, 66, 68, 70) sts.

Work even until sleeve measures 38 (39, 39, 39, 40, 40) cm [15 (15¼, 15¼, 15¼, 15¾, 15¾) in.], ending with WS row.

Shape sleevehead

Cast off 6 (6, 7, 7, 8, 8) sts at beg of next 2 rows: 48 (50, 50, 52, 52, 54) sts.

Dec 1 st at each end of next 3 rows, then on every other row once, then on every foll 4th row until 32 (34, 34, 36, 36, 38) sts rem.

Work 1 row even.

Dec 1 st at each end of next row and on every other row 1 (2, 2, 3, 3, 4) times, and then on 5 foll rows.

Cast off rem 18 sts.

FINISHING

Press as described on page 21.

Join right shoulder seam.

Make neckband

With RS facing and using 4¹/₂ mm (US 7) needles, pick up and knit 15 (15, 15, 18, 18, 18) sts down left front neck, 16 sts across centre front, 15 (15, 15, 18, 18, 18) sts up right front neck, and 30 (30, 30, 32, 32, 32) sts across back neck: 76 (76, 76, 84, 84, 84) sts.

Next row (WS): *K2, P2, rep from * to last 2 sts, K2.

Next row: *P2, K2, rep from * to last 2 sts, P2.

These 2 rows form rib.

Work until rib measures 10 cm (4 in.).

Cast off in rib.

Join left shoulder and neckband seam.

Join side and sleeve seams.

Match centre of cast off edge to shoulder seam.

Set-in sleeve, easing sleevehead into armhole.

Make cable edging

Using 4¹/₂ mm (US 7) needles, cast on 12 sts and work from chart (opposite) and written instructions as folls:

Chart row 1 (RS): K1, P1, K6, [P1, K1] twice.

Chart row 2: [K1, P1] twice, K1, P6, K1.

Work 8 more rows in patt from chart.

Chart row 11: K1, P1, C10B.

Chart row 12: P5, [K1, P1] 3 times, K1.

Work 8 more rows in patt from chart.

Chart row 21: K1, P1, C10B.

Chart row 22: [K1, P1] twice, K1, P6, K1.

Work 8 more rows in patt from chart.

Rep rows 11-30 until cable edging fits neatly around lower edge of sweater without stretching.

Cast off.

Slip stitch cast-on and cast off edges neatly together to form a circle and then, matching the seam with right seam, slip stitch the straight (moss st) edge side of the cable neatly in place around the lower edge of the sweater.

Work two more lengths of edging, each long enough to fit around lower edge of the sleeves.

Slip stitch cast-on and cast off edges neatly together to form a circle and then, matching the seams, slip stitch the straight edge of the cable neatly in place around the cuff edge of each sleeve.

cable-and-lace sweater

To fit bust size:

81	86	91	97	102	107 cm
32	**34**	**36**	**38**	**40**	**42 in.**

Actual width at underarm (A):

99	103	109	112	118	122 cm
39	**40¹/₂**	**43**	**44**	**46¹/₂**	**48 in.**

Finished length (B):

51	51	54	54	57	57 cm
20	**20**	**21¹/₄**	**21¹/₄**	**22¹/₂**	**22¹/₂ in.**

Sleeve length to underarm (C):

46	46	47	47	48	48 cm
18	**18**	**18¹/₂**	**18¹/₂**	**19**	**19 in.**

YARN

50g balls of Kashmir Aran (Merino/cashmere/microfibre), #5 Sea Green:

14	15	16	17	18	19

NEEDLES

Pair of 4¹/₂ mm (US 7) knitting needles
Pair of 5 mm (US 8) knitting needles
Cable needle

TENSION

21 sts and 24 rows = 10 cm (4 in.) square measured over cable patt using 5 mm (US 8) knitting needles.

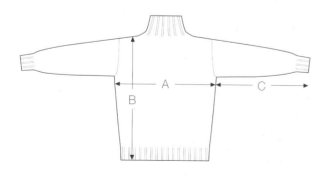

Traditional Aran sweaters have patterns handed down for generations. Here is a design combining time-honoured cables with a pretty lace stitch.

BACK

Using 4¹/₂ mm (US 7) needles, cast on 104 (108, 114, 118, 124, 128) sts.

Next row (RS): K1 (1, 0, 0, 1, 1), *P2, K2, rep from * to last 3 (3, 2, 2, 3, 3) sts, P2, K1 (1, 0, 0, 1, 1).

Next row: P1 (1, 0, 0, 1, 1), *K2, P2, rep from * to last 3 (3, 2, 2, 3, 3) sts, K2, P1 (1, 0, 0, 1, 1).

These 2 rows form rib.

Work in rib for a further 12 rows, ending with WS row.

Change to 5 mm (US 8) needles and work from Back and Front chart on page 105 as folls:

Next row (RS): P6 (8, 11, 13, 16, 18), work next 92 sts from chart row 1, P6 (8, 11, 13, 16, 18).

Next row: K6 (8, 11, 13, 16, 18), work next 92 sts from chart row 2, K6 (8, 11, 13, 16, 18).

These 2 rows set the sts.

Cont in patt until work measures 32 (32, 34, 34, 36, 36) cm [12¹/₂ (12¹/₂, 13¹/₂, 13¹/₂, 14¹/₄, 14¹/₄) in], ending with WS row.

Shape armholes

Cast off 6 (6, 7, 7, 8, 8) sts at beg next 2 rows, then 4 (4, 5, 5, 6, 6) sts at beg foll 2 rows: 84 (88, 90, 94, 96, 100) sts.

Dec 1 st at each end of next row and then every other row 4 (5, 5, 6, 6, 7) times: 74 (76, 78, 80, 82, 84) sts.

Work even until armhole measures 19 (19, 20, 20, 21, 21) cm [7¹/₂ (7¹/₂, 8, 8, 8¹/₄, 8¹/₄) in.], ending with RS facing for next row.

Shape shoulders and back neck

Cast on 6 (6, 6, 6, 7, 7) sts at beg of next 2 rows: 62 (64, 66, 68, 68, 70) sts.

Next row (RS): Cast off 6 (6, 6, 6, 7, 7) sts at beg of next row, patt until there are 9 (10, 11, 11, 10, 11) sts on RH needle and turn, place rem sts on a holder.

Work both sides of neck separately.

Cast off 4 sts, purl to end.

Cast off rem 5 (6, 7, 7, 6, 7) sts.

With RS facing, rejoin yarn to sts from holder, cast off centre 32 (32, 32, 34, 34, 34) sts, work in patt to end.

Complete to match first side, reversing shaping.

FRONT

Work as for back until you have worked 12 (12, 12, 14, 14, 14) rows fewer than on back to start of shoulder shaping, ending with WS row.

Shape neck

Next row (RS): Work 25 (26, 27, 28, 29, 30) and turn, place rem sts on a holder.

Cast off 4 sts at beg of next row.

Dec 1 st at neck edge on next 4 rows, then on every other row 0 (0, 0, 1, 1, 1) times: 17 (18, 19, 19, 20, 21) sts rem.

Cont straight until front matches back to beg of shoulder shaping, ending with WS row.

Shape shoulder

Cast off 6 (6, 6, 6, 7, 7) sts at beg of next 2 RS rows.

Work 1 row even.

Cast off rem 5 (6, 7, 7, 6, 7) sts.

With RS facing, rejoin yarn to sts from holder, cast off centre 24 sts, work in patt to end.

Complete to match first side, reversing shaping.

SLEEVES (work both the same)

Using 4¹⁄₂ mm (US 7) needles, cast off 52 (52, 54, 54, 56, 56) sts.

Next row (RS): K1 (1, 0, 0, 1, 1), *P2, K2, rep from * to last 3 (3 ,2, 2, 3, 3) sts, P2, K1 (1, 0, 0, 1, 1).

Next row: P1 (1, 0, 0, 1, 1), *K2, purl, rep from * to last 3 (3, 2, 2, 3, 3) sts, K2, P1 (1, 0, 0, 1, 1).

These 2 rows form rib.

Work in rib for a further 12 rows, inc 1 st at centre of last row, and ending with RS facing for next row: 53 (53, 55, 55, 57, 57) sts.

Change to 5 mm (US 8) needles and work in Sleeve chart, opposite, as folls:

Next row (RS): P0 (0, 1, 1, 2, 2), work next 53 sts in patt from chart row 1, P0 (0, 1, 1, 2, 2).

Next row: K0 (0, 1, 1, 2, 2), work next 53 sts in patt from chart row 2, K0 (0, 1, 1, 2, 2).

These 2 rows est patt.

Cont in patt, inc 1 st at each end of next row and every foll 18th (18th, 18th, 18th, 20th, 20th) row to 63 (63, 65, 65, 67, 67) sts, working inc sts in rev st st.

Work even until sleeve measures 46 (46, 47, 47, 48, 48) cm [18 (18, 18¹⁄₂, 18¹⁄₂, 19, 19) in.], ending with WS row.

Shape sleevehead

Cast off 5 sts at beg next 2 rows: 53 (53, 55, 55, 57, 57) sts.

Dec 1 st at each end of next 3 rows, then on every other row 3 times, and then on every foll 4th row until 35 sts rem.

Work 1 row even.

Dec 1 st at each end of next 2 RS rows, then on 3 foll rows.

Cast off 3 sts at beg of next 4 rows.

Cast off rem 13 sts.

FINISHING

Press as described on page 21.

Join right shoulder seam.

Make neckband

With RS facing and using 4¹/₂ mm (US 7) needles, pick up and knit 16 (16, 16, 18, 18, 18) sts down left front neck, 24 sts across centre front, 16 (16, 16, 18, 18, 18) sts up right front neck, and 40 (40, 40, 44, 44, 44) sts across back neck: 96 (96, 96, 104, 104, 104) sts.

Next row (WS): *K2, P2, rep from * to end.

Next row: *K2, P2, rep from * to end.

These 2 rows form rib.

Work in rib for a further 12 rows, and cast off in rib.

Cast off in rib.

Join left shoulder and neckband seam.

Join side and sleeve seams.

Match centre of cast off edge to shoulder seam.

Set in sleeve, easing sleevehead into armhole.

Back & Front Chart

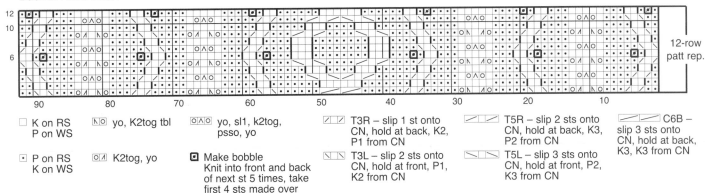

☐ K on RS
P on WS

⊡ P on RS
K on WS

⊠ yo, K2tog tbl

⊡ K2tog, yo

○∧○ yo, sl1, k2tog, psso, yo

⊡ Make bobble
Knit into front and back of next st 5 times, take first 4 sts made over last st.

T3R – slip 1 st onto CN, hold at back, K2, P1 from CN

T3L – slip 2 sts onto CN, hold at front, P1, K2 from CN

T5R – slip 2 sts onto CN, hold at back, K3, P2 from CN

T5L – slip 3 sts onto CN, hold at front, P2, K3 from CN

C6B – slip 3 sts onto CN, hold at back, K3, K3 from CN

Sleeve Chart

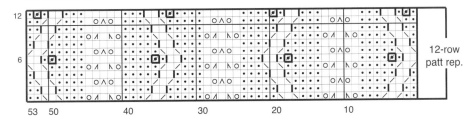

cable pullover

To fit bust size:					
81	86	91	97	102	107 cm
32	**34**	**36**	**38**	**40**	**42 in.**
Actual width at underarm (A):					
86	91	97	102	108	113 cm
34	**35³/₄**	**38**	**40**	**42¹/₂**	**44¹/₂ in.**
Finished length (B):					
55	56	57	58	59	60 cm
21³/₄	**22**	**22¹/₂**	**22³/₄**	**23¹/₄**	**23¹/₂ in.**
Sleeve length to underarm (C):					
44	45	45	45	46	46 cm
17¹/₄	**17³/₄**	**17³/₄**	**17³/₄**	**18**	**18 in.**

YARN

50g balls of Kashmir Aran (Merino/cashmere/microfibre),
#2 Blue:

13	13	14	14	15	15

NEEDLES

Pair of 4¹/₂ mm (US 7) knitting needles
Pair of 5 mm (US 8) knitting needles
Cable needle

TENSION

18 sts and 24 rows = 10 cm (4in.) square measured over
st st using 5 mm (US 8) knitting needles.

The single dramatic cable on the front of this simple
sweater runs right up onto the ribbed neck, creating
an eyecatching feature.

BACK

Using 4¹/₂ mm (US 7) needles, cast on 78 (82, 90, 94, 98, 102)
sts.

Next row (RS): *K2, P2, rep from * to last 2 sts, K2.

Next row: *P2, K2, rep from * to last 2 sts, P2.

Rep these 2 rows 4 times more, dec 0 (0, 1, 1, 0, 0) sts at
each end of last row, ending with WS row: 78 (82, 88, 92, 98,
102) sts.

Change to 5 mm (US 8) needles and, beg with a knit row,
work in st st as folls:

Dec 1 st at each end of 3rd row and every foll 6th row until
70 (74, 80, 84, 90, 94) sts rem.

Work 11 (13, 13, 15, 15, 17) rows even, ending with WS row.

Inc 1 st at each end of next row and every foll 10th row until
there are 78 (82, 88, 92, 98, 102) sts.

Work even until work measures 35 (36, 36, 37, 37, 38) cm
[13³/₄ (14¹/₄, 14¹/₄, 14¹/₂, 14¹/₂, 15) in], ending with WS row.

Shape armholes

Cast off 5 (6, 6, 7, 7, 8) sts at beg of next 2 rows: 68 (70, 76,
78, 84, 86) sts.

Dec 1 st at each end of next 3 (3, 5, 5, 7, 7) rows, then on
next RS row once: 60 (62, 64, 66, 68, 70) sts.

Work without further shaping until armhole measures 20 (20,
21, 21, 22, 22) cm [8 (8, 8¹/₄, 8¹/₄, 8³/₄, 8³/₄) in.], ending with
WS row.

Shape shoulders and back neck

Cast off 5 (5, 6, 6, 6, 6) sts at beg of next 2 rows: 50 (52, 52,
54, 56, 58) sts.

Next row (RS): Cast off 5 (5, 6, 6, 6, 6) sts at beg of next row,
knit until there are 8 (9, 8, 8, 9, 10) sts on RH needle and turn,
place rem sts on a holder.

Work both sides of neck separately.

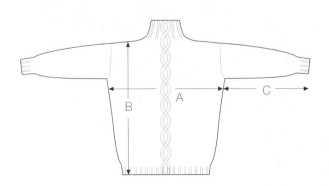

Cable Panel Chart

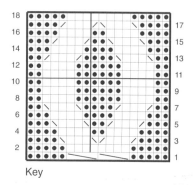

18-row
patt rep.

Key

☐ K on RS, P on WS

▣ P on RS, K on WS

Cr4R — sl next st to cable needle, hold at back of work, KR, then P1 from cable needle.

Cr4L — sl next 4 sts to cable needle, hold at front of work, P1, then K4 from cable needle.

C8F — sl next 4 sts to cable needle, K4, then K4 from cable needle.

Cast off 3 sts, purl to end.

Cast off rem 5 (6, 5, 5, 6, 7) sts.

With RS facing, rejoin yarn to sts from holder, and cast off centre 24 (24, 24, 26, 26, 26) sts, knit to end.

Complete to match first side, reversing shaping and working an extra row before beg of shoulder shaping.

FRONT

Using 4½ mm (US 7) needles, cast on 82 (86, 92, 96, 102, 106) sts.

Next row (RS): P0 (0, 0, 1, 0, 0), K0 (2, 1, 2, 2, 0), (P2, K2) 8 (8, 9, 9, 10, 11) times, work row 1 of chart, (K2, P2) 8 (8, 9, 9, 10, 11) times, K0 (2, 1, 2, 2, 0), P0 (0, 0, 1, 0, 0).

Next row: K0 (0, 0, 1, 0, 0), P0 (2, 1, 2, 2, 0), (K2, P2) 8 (8, 9, 9, 10, 11) times, work row 2 of chart, (P2, K2) 8 (8, 9, 9, 10, 11) times, P0 (2, 1, 2, 2, 0), K0 (0, 0, 1, 0, 0).

Rep these 2 rows 4 times more, working across rows 3-10 of chart, ending with WS row.

Change to 5 mm (US 8) needles and cont in cable patt as folls:

Next row (RS): K32 (34, 37, 39, 42, 44), work chart row 11, knit to end.

Next row: P32 (34, 37, 39, 42, 44), work chart row 12, purl to end.

These 2 rows set position of cable panel.

Keeping patt correct, cont as folls:

Dec 1 st at each end of next row and every foll 6th row until 74 (78, 84, 88, 94, 98) sts rem.

Work 11 (13, 13, 15, 15, 17) rows even, ending with WS row.

Inc 1 st at each end of next row and every foll 10th row until there are 82 (86, 92, 96, 102, 106) sts.

Work even until front measures same as back to beg of armhole shaping, ending with WS row.

Shape armholes

Keeping in patt, cast off 5 (6, 6, 7, 7, 8) sts at beg of next 2 rows: 72 (74, 80, 82, 88, 90) sts.

Dec 1 st at each end of next 3 (3, 5, 5, 7, 7) rows, then on foll RS row: 64 (66, 68, 70, 72, 74) sts.

Work even until you have worked 14 (14, 14, 16, 16, 16) rows fewer than on back to start of shoulder shaping, ending with WS row.

Shape neck

Next row (RS): K22 (23, 24, 25, 26, 27) and turn, place rem sts on a holder.

Dec 1 st at neck edge on next 4 rows, then on every other row 2 (2, 2, 3, 3, 3) times, and then on every foll 4th row until 15 (16, 17, 17, 18, 19) sts rem.

Work even until front matches back to beg of shoulder shaping, ending with WS row.

Shape shoulder

Cast off 5 (5, 6, 6, 6, 6) sts at beg of next 2 RS rows.

Work 1 row even.

Cast off rem 5 (6, 5, 5, 6, 7) sts.

With RS facing, slip centre 20 sts on holder, rejoin yarn to sts from first holder, knit to end.

Complete to match first side, reversing shaping and working an extra row before start of shoulder shaping.

SLEEVES (work both the same)

Using 4½ mm (US 7) needles, cast on 42 (42, 42, 42, 42, 46) sts.

Next row (RS): *K2, P2, rep from * to last 2 sts, K2.

Next row: *P2, K2, rep from * to last 2 sts, P2.

Rep these 2 rows 4 times more, dec 0 (0, 1, 1, 1, 0) sts at each end of last row, and ending with WS row: 42 (42, 44, 44, 44, 46) sts.

Change to 5 mm (US 8) needles and, beg with a knit row, work in st st, inc 1 st at each end of 3rd and every foll 12th (10th, 10th, 8th, 8th, 8th) row to 46 (58, 60, 66, 66, 68) sts, then on

every foll 10th (8th, 8th, –, 6th, 6th) row until there are 60 (62, 64, 66, 68, 70) sts.

Work without further shaping until sleeve measures 44 (45, 45, 45, 46, 46) cm [17¼ (17¾, 17¾, 17¾, 18, 18) in], ending with WS row.

Shape sleevehead

Cast off 5 (6, 6, 7, 7, 8) sts at beg of next 2 rows: 50 (50, 52, 52, 54, 54) sts.

Dec 1 st at each end of next 3 rows, then on every other row twice, and then on every foll 4th row until 34 (34, 36, 36, 38, 38) sts rem.

Work 1 row even.

Dec 1 st at each end of next row and then on every other row 1 (1, 2, 2, 3, 3) time, and then on 5 foll rows.

Cast off 4 sts at beg of next 2 rows.

Cast off rem 12 sts.

FINISHING

Press as described on page 21.

Join right shoulder seam.

Make collar

With RS facing and using 4½ mm (US 7) needles, pick up and knit 19 (19, 19, 21, 21, 21) sts down left front neck, work in patt across 20 sts from front holder, pick up and knit 19 (19, 19, 21, 21, 21) sts up right front neck, and 30 (30, 30, 32, 32, 32) sts across back: 88 (88, 88, 94, 94, 94) sts.

Next row (WS): P2, (K2, P2) 12 (12, 12, 13, 13, 13) times, work in patt from chart across next 18 sts, (P2, K2) to last 0 (0, 0, 2, 2, 2) sts, P0 (0, 0, 2, 2, 2).

Working patt as est, cont in rib with centre cable panel until collar measures 10 cm (4 in.).

Cast off in patt.

Join left shoulder and collar seam.

Join side and sleeve seams.

Match centre of cast off edge to shoulder seam.

Set in sleeve, easing sleevehead into armhole.

textured heart sweater

To fit bust size:					
81	86	91	97	102	107 cm
32	**34**	**36**	**38**	**40**	**42 in.**
Actual width at underarm (A):					
90	97	101	108	112	119 cm
35¹/₂	**38¹/₄**	**39³/₄**	**42¹/₂**	**44**	**46³/₄ in.**
Finished length (B):					
52	53	54	55	56	57 cm
20¹/₂	**20³/₄**	**21¹/₄**	**21³/₄**	**22**	**22¹/₂ in.**
Sleeve length to underarm (C):					
44	45	45	45	46	46 cm
17¹/₄	**17³/₄**	**17³/₄**	**17³/₄**	**18**	**18 in.**

YARN

50g balls of Kashmir Aran (Merino/cashmere/microfiber), #3 Rose:

14	15	15	16	16	17

NEEDLES

Pair of 4¹/₂ mm (US 7) knitting needles
Pair of 5 mm (US 8) knitting needles
Cable needle

TENSION

18 sts and 24 rows = 10 cm (4 in.) square measured over st st using 5 mm (US 8) knitting needles.

What could be more feminine than the row of pretty hearts on this cropped sweater? The lattice work on either side looks intricate but is quite easy to knit.

BACK

Using 4¹/₂ mm (US 7) needles, cast on 90 (94, 98, 106, 110, 114) sts.

Next row (RS): *K2, P2, rep from * to last 2 sts, K2.

Next row: *P2, K2, rep from * to last 2 sts, P2.

Rep these 2 rows 4 times more, dec (inc, inc, dec, dec, inc) 1 st at end of last row, and ending with RS facing for next row: 89 (95, 99, 105, 109, 115).

Change to 5 mm (US 8) needles and work in patt as folls:

Next row (RS): K0 (1, 1, 0, 0, 1), (P1, K1) 5 (6, 7, 9, 10, 11) times, work across row 1 of Front and Back chart (page 120), (K1, P1) 5 (6, 7, 9, 10, 11) times, K0 (1, 1, 0, 0, 1).

Next row: K0 (1, 1, 0, 0, 1), (P1, K1) 5 (6, 7, 9, 10, 11) times, work across row 2 of chart, (K1, P1) 5 (6, 7, 9, 10, 11) times, K0 (1, 1, 0, 0, 1).

These 2 rows set position of chart with seed stitch borders.

Cont in patt as set, work even until work measures 32 (33, 33, 34, 34, 35) cm [12¹/₂ (13, 13, 13¹/₂, 13¹/₂, 13³/₄) in.], ending with WS row.

Shape armholes

Cast off 6 (6, 7, 7, 8, 8) sts at beg of next 2 rows: 77 (83, 85, 91, 93, 99) sts.

Dec 1 st at each end of next 3 (5, 5, 7, 7, 9) rows, then on every other row twice: 67 (69, 71, 73, 75, 77) sts.

Work even until armhole measures 20 (20, 21, 21, 22, 22) cm [8 (8, 8¹/₄, 8¹/₄, 8³/₄, 8³/₄) in., ending with WS row.

Shape shoulders and back neck

Keeping in patt, cast off 5 (6, 6, 6, 6, 7) sts at beg of next 2 rows: 57 (57, 59, 61, 63, 63) sts.

Next row (RS): BO 5 (6, 6, 6, 6, 7) sts at beg of row, working in patt until there are 9 (8, 9, 9, 10, 9) sts on RH needle and turn, place rem sts on a holder.

Front & Back Chart

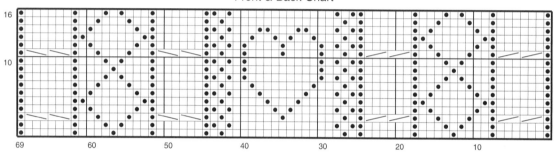

16-row
patt rep.

Sleeve Chart

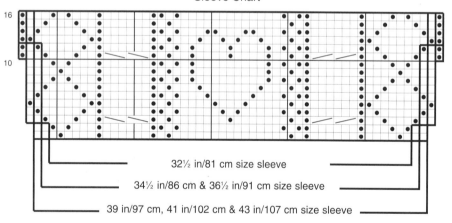

16-row
patt rep.

32½ in/81 cm size sleeve

34½ in/86 cm & 36½ in/91 cm size sleeve

39 in/97 cm, 41 in/102 cm & 43 in/107 cm size sleeve

Key

☐ K on RS, P on WS

▣ P on RS, K on WS

C6B - slip next 3 sts on cable needle and hold at back of work K3, then K3 from cable needle.

C6F - slip next 3 sts on cable needle and hold at back of work K3, then K3 from cable needle.

Work both sides of neck separately.

Cast off 3 sts, work in patt to end.

Cast off rem 6 (5, 6, 6, 7, 6) sts.

With RS facing, rejoin yarn to sts from holder and cast off centre 29 (29, 29, 31, 31, 31) sts, work in patt to end.

Complete to match first side, reversing shaping and working an extra row before beg of shoulder shaping.

FRONT

Work as for back until you have worked 14 (14, 14, 16, 16, 16) rows fewer than on back to start of shoulder shaping, ending with WS row.

Shape neck

Next row (RS): Work 25 (26, 27, 28, 29, 30) sts and turn, place rem sts on a holder.

Dec 1 st at neck edge on next 6 rows, then on every other row 3 (3, 3, 4, 4, 4) times, and then on every foll 4th row until 16 (17, 18, 18, 19, 20) sts rem.

Work even until front matches back to beg of shoulder shaping, ending with WS row.

Shape shoulder

Cast off 5 (6, 6, 6, 6, 7) sts at beg of next 2 RS rows.

Work 1 row even.

Cast off rem 6 (5, 6, 6, 7, 6) sts.

With RS facing, rejoin yarn to sts from holder and cast off centre 17 sts, work in patt to end.

Complete to match first side, reversing shaping.

SLEEVES (work both the same)

Using 4 1/2 mm (US 7) needles, cast off 46 (50, 50, 50, 50, 50) sts.

Next row (RS): *K2, P2, rep from * to last 2 sts, K2.

Next row: *P2, K2, rep from * to last 2 sts, P2.

Rep these 2 rows 4 times more, inc (dec, dec, inc, inc, inc) 1 st at end of last row, ending with WS row: 47 (49, 49, 51, 51, 51) sts.

Change to 5 mm (US 8) needles and work in patt from sleeve chart (opposite), inc 1 st at each end of 3rd and every foll 10th (10th, 10th, 10th, 8th, 8th) row to 59 (63, 55, 57, 73, 67)sts, then on every foll 8th (8th, 8th, 8th, 6th, 6th) row until there are 67 (69, 71, 73, 75, 77) sts, working inc sts in seed st after the 55 chart sts have been achieved.

Work without further shaping until sleeve measures 44 (45, 45, 45, 46, 46) cm [17 1/4 (17 3/4, 17 3/4, 17 3/4, 18, 18) in], ending with WS row.

Shape sleevehead

Cast off 6 (6, 7, 7, 8, 8) sts at beg of next 2 rows: 55 (57, 57, 59, 59, 61) sts.

Dec 1 st at each end of next 5 rows, then on foll RS row, then on every foll 4th row until 37 (39, 39, 41, 41, 43) sts rem.

Work 1 row even.

Dec 1 st at each end of next row and on every other row 1 (1, 2, 2, 3, 3) times, and then on 5 foll rows.

Every other row 5 sts at beg of next 2 rows.

Cast off rem 13 (15, 13, 15, 13, 15) sts.

FINISHING

Press as described on page 21.

Join shoulder seams.

Make collar

Using 4 1/2 mm (US 7) needles, cast on 98 (98, 98, 106, 106, 106) sts.

Next row (RS): *K2, P2, rep from * to last 2 sts, K2.

Next row: *P2, K2, rep from * to last 2 sts, P2.

Rep these 2 rows until collar measures 5 in. (13 cm).

Cast off evenly in rib.

Sew bound-off edge of collar in place, overlapping edges at centre front.

Join side and sleeve seams.

Match centre of bound-off edge to shoulder seam.

Set in sleeve, easing sleevehead into armhole.

abbreviations

Check your chosen project as you may find a special abbreviation note. Some of the most common words used have been abbreviated as listed below:

alt	alternate
approx	approximately
beg	begin(ning)
CC	contrasting color
cm	centimetres
cont	continue
dec	decreas(e)(ing)
dpn	double-pointed needles
foll	follow(ing)
garter st	garter stitch (knit every row)
in	inch(es)
inc	increase(e)(ing)
K	knit
kw	knitwise
K2tog	knit two sts together
LH	left hand (needle)
P	purl
P2tog	purl two sts together
patt	pattern
psso	pass slip stich over
pw	purlwise
rem	remain(ing)
rep	repeat
rnd	round
rev	reverse(ing)
RH	right hand (needle)
RS	right side
Sl1	slip 1 stitch
St st	stockinette stitch
st(s)	stitches
tbl	through back of loop
tog	together

WS	wrong side
YO	yarn over/forward

US GLOSSRY	UK GLOSSARY
Bind off	Cast off
Gauge	Tension
Stockinette stitch	Stocking stitch
Seed stitch	Moss stitch

SPECIAL ABBREVIATIONS

C6B	slip next 3 sts on to cable needle and hold at back of work, K3, then K3 from cable needle.
C6F	slip next 3 sts on to cable needle and hold at front of work, K3, then K3 from cable needle.
C8F	slip next 4 sts on to cable needle and hold at front of work, K4, then K4 from cable needle.
C10B	slip next 5 sts on to cable needle and hold at back of work, (K1, P1) twice, K1, then K5 from cable needle.
Cr4L	slip next 4 sts on to cable needle and hold at front of work, P1, then K4 from cable needle.
Cr4R	slip next st on to cable needle and hold at back of work, K4, then P1 from cable needle.
MB	make bobble (on WS): K into front, back, front, back, then front again of next st, lift 2nd, 3rd, 4th, and 5th sts on right needle over first st and off needle.

project index

fitted turtleneck
sweater p24

cropped basic
sweater p32

fitted v-neck sweater
p24

simple v-neck
cardigan p38

fitted short-sleeved
sweater p24

lace v-neck
cardigan p38

long basic sweater
p32

lace cardigan p44

 fitted angora sweater
p50

 nautical stripe p66

 fitted mohair sweater
p50

 shawl-collar jacket
p72

 lace vest p58

 fair isle sweater p76

 twin set p60

 fitted cardigan p80

panel jacket p84

cable-edged tunic
p104

sloppy joe p90

cable-and-lace
sweater p108

relaxed cardigan p94

cable pullover p112

longline jacket p100

textured heart sweater
p116

Louisa Harding yarns

Featured Yarns

Angora (Kimono Angora Pure)
70% Angora, 25% wool, 5% Nylon,
25g ball, each approx 125 yds (114 m)
Double Knitting
Pure colour

Fauve
100% Nylon
50g ball, each approx 80 m (87 yds)
Cotton weight

Impression
16% Mohair, 84% Polymide
50g ball, each approx 141 m (154 yds)
Double Knitting

Kashmir Aran
55% Merino Wool, 10% Cashmere,
35% Microfibre
50g ball, each approx 75 m (83 yds)
Aran

Kashmir DK
55% Merino Wool, 10% Cashmere,
35% Microfibre
50g ball, each approx 105 m (116 yds)
Double Knitting

Kimono Angora
70% Angora, 25% wool, 5% Nylon
25g ball, each approx 114 m (125 yds).

Double Knitting
Variegated shades

Kimono Ribbon
100% Nylon
50g ball, each approx 102 yds (93 m)

Nautical Cotton
100% Mercerized Cotton
50g ball, each approx 85 m (93 yds)
Cotton

Distributors

United Kingdom
Designer Yarns LTD
Units 8-10 Newbridge Industrial Estate,
Pitt Street, Keighley, West Yorkshire BD21
4PQ
TEL: 44 (0) 1535 664222
FAX: 44 (0) 1535 664333
www.designeryarns.uk.com
david@designeryarns.uk.com

USA
EuroYarns
315 Bayview Avenue
Amityville, NY 11701
TEL: (516) 546-3600 FAX: (516) 546-6871
www.euroyarns.com
admin@knittingfever.com

Canada
Diamond Yarns LTD
155 Martain Ross Ave. Unit 3,
Toronto, Ontario M3J 2L9
Tel: (416) 736-6111
www.diamondyarn.com
diamond@diamondyarn.com

acknowledgments

For Belle & Oscar, thankfully children change everything.

This book would not be possible without the help of the following people; Stephen Jessup, my rock; Granny Daph, Nana Carole and Auntie Di Di; My wonderful knitters, Betty Rothwell, Mrs. Marsh, Daphne Harding, Mary Butler, Beryl White, Mrs. Wilmot, and Janet Mann.

Thank you to Stella Smith, who worked with me writing and checking the patterns in this book, helping me create such beautiful designs.

Finally, thank you to the team at Collins & Brown for making this book a reality.